T0208483

*"Jennifer Blair's new must-read book, **The True You Reimagined**, will guide you through your own uncovering and discovering who you were always meant to be-- your authentic self-- but needed a roadmap to get there. Jennifer Blair in her wisdom takes you to that very place."*
Albert Gaulden, Founding Director, The Sedona Intensive

*"Jennifer's messages of motivation and mindfulness make **The True You Reimagined** a useful companion to achieving and maintaining your desired life. Her relaxed, friendly style makes reading the book feel like a wonderful pep talk from a wise and well-meaning friend."*
Sarah Ivens, Best-selling author of *Forest Therapy: Seasonal Ways to Embrace Nature for a Happier You!*

*"I have received Jennifer's monthly newsletters for years and have found them to be extremely useful and inspiring. **The True You Reimagined** is a must read for anyone who is looking to improve their life as well as those around them!*
Christine Klote, Chief Operating Officer at Structural Steel Products

*"Jennifer is life changing. I started coaching with Jennifer in 2005, and she has made a compelling impact on my life. As a result, I'm successful, I'm happy, and I'm a powerful! Jennifer's book is an inspiring and easy-to-read guide for unleashing your truest self. It's a collection of creatively written wisdoms, bundled into simple life themes that are an empowering guide for you to achieve more success in life, gain insights around a topic, and excavate your best potential. Use **The True You Reimagined** to unlock your truest self."*
Susan Lampinen, Group Chief Designer— Color + Material Design, Ford Motor Company

*"I worked years for the Department of the Army, traveling the world, and always carried with me Jennifer's book, **The True You** EVERYWHERE! It's been all over the globe and has been a lifesaver to me. Encouraging when I need it and reminding me, I am human. **The True You** is truly my favorite book and I've given it as a gift to so many. Thank you for what you do, you make the world a better place by your being."*
Tammy Bryson Quetot, Social Worker

*"Jennifer was instrumental in the success of Underwired publication for 6 ½ years— as my Life Coach, a contributing writer, inspirational speaker for our 'Wired and Inspired' events and model for how she lives her own life. I know that you will feel inspired while reading **this book**."*
Laura Grinstead, Publisher of the former *Underwired* Magazine

*"For the past several years, I have greatly enjoyed a relationship with Jennifer as a coach to help me build and maintain my business, and my firm has even utilized her to conduct company-wide workshops. Why do I love working with Jennifer? She's not just a coach, but also your biggest cheerleader."*
Reed B. Weinberg, President, PRG | Commercial Property Advisors

*"**The True You** helped me discover my core values and prioritize my life so that I stay true to what's important in my life. This experience has been life changing."*
Teresa Oechsli, Executive Director/Founder, Hosea's House Inc.

*"I've known Jennifer since 2006 when we were engaged in a year-long leadership program offered by CTI, the premier coaching company that trained us. As a result of that intimate and intense experience I came to know Jennifer as a woman who walks the talk of her beliefs as a coach. She participated in that program from a place of unwavering authenticity, living fully aligned with her values and as generous of spirit as a person could be. I am honored to have her as a colleague and a friend."*
Susan Bedsow Horgan**,** President, Making Peace With Potato Chips, LLC

*"Jennifer is incredibly smart! She is insightful, listens both firmly and empathetically, challenges you to be your best. She has systems, is organized, keeps great notes and really gets into your mission. She makes you feel like she's your best friend who demands more of you...which is why you hire her in the first place! My life has improved because of my work with Jennifer. Get her on your team! She's worth it... and so are you!"*
Liz McGovern, Principal, Liz McGovern & Associates

*"Jennifer Blair is lively, sensitive and insightful. She asks the right questions and provides suggestions that are consistently thoughtful, helpful and reflective*

*of the best in contemporary life coaching. She is an effective model for wit, style and resiliency, and her book,* **The True You,** *is a compilation of her best work."*

Anita P. Barbee, MSSW, Ph.D. Professor and
Distinguished University Scholar,
Kent School of Social Work University of Louisville

*"Jennifer Blair is an immensely gifted coach. As her client, she has guided me to positive changes that permeate my life, encouraging life balance, personal growth and illuminating the path to finding my passion. Her true talent is her ability to lead people to a mindset that develops their very best, while addressing key patterns that serve as obstacles to growth. Empowered with a wealth of tools that support her clients' vision and a steady stream of follow up, compassion, accountability and wisdom, she truly finds joy in every aspect of her work. I often say, she is the coach with the most and an inspirational force."*

Heather Mickley, Marketing and Communications Manager
at Spirit Rock - An Insight Meditation Center

*"Jennifer's coaching has been transformational for my life. With insight and empathy, she is able to guide me past personal roadblocks and motivate me beyond my preconceptions. Working with Jennifer, I've gained deep insight into my own skills, talents, desires and purpose, which has guided me to better relationships, more satisfying work, and an overall sense of deep satisfaction with my life and the trajectory I am on. I plan to utilize her coaching throughout my life to continue designing the life I desire."*

Kim Martin, Founder, KMD, LLC

# THE TRUE YOU REIMAGINED

## Discover
### *Your Authentic Self*

JENNIFER BLAIR

# THE TRUE YOU REIMAGINED
## DISCOVER YOUR AUTHENTIC SELF

*iUniverse books may be ordered through booksellers or by contacting:*

*iUniverse*
*1663 Liberty Drive*
*Bloomington, IN 47403*
*www.iuniverse.com*
*1-800-Authors (1-800-288-4677)*

*Because of the dynamic nature of the Internet, any web addresses or links contained in this book may have changed since publication and may no longer be valid. The views expressed in this work are solely those of the author and do not necessarily reflect the views of the publisher, and the publisher hereby disclaims any responsibility for them.*

*Any people depicted in stock imagery provided by Getty Images are models, and such images are being used for illustrative purposes only.*
*Certain stock imagery © Getty Images.*

*ISBN: 978-1-6632-0063-1 (sc)*
*ISBN: 978-1-6632-0064-8 (e)*

*Library of Congress Control Number: 2020909617*

*Print information available on the last page.*

*iUniverse rev. date: 06/05/2020*

*To my incredible children with much love, Taylor and Tess. You amazingly remain true to yourselves and have discovered how to be beautiful adults... I am in awe.*

# Contents

*Many of the following chapters are from my Evolve columns published in Underwired Magazine in Louisville, Kentucky, from May 2007-December 2012 which have been updated, re-written and evolved. Also included is new material I have created over the past eight years.*

## Uncover Your Authenticity

## Cultivate Balance & Being

## Pursue Passion & Play

## Enhance Your Work

## Enrich Your Relationships

## Break Free

## Appendix

# Acknowledgements

There are many people who have supported me in writing this book over the past few years. Some are still in my life, others have moved on… but to everyone, I am eternally blessed by having experienced you. With deep gratitude and appreciation, I want to directly thank the following for their encouragement, love and support.

The writing opportunity: I am forever grateful to Laura Grinstead, publisher *Underwired* magazine, who gave me the writing opportunity to create and write a monthly Life Coaching column called Evolve starting in 2007. You created such a beautiful magazine that encouraged women to pursue their meaningful work and other passionate endeavors. I appreciated the chance to inspire these women and to continually raise the bar on my creativity.

My amazing support team: My assistant of 14 years, Meredith Williams keeps me organized— much love to you. My graphic designers, Natalie McGuire who makes me and my brand beautiful and Natalie Biesel who translates my coaching ideas into visually useful exercises and materials, many thanks to you both. A special note of gratitude for James Melcher, my sometimes coach and always friend, I love that we have remained close.

My soulful supporters: To my sister and best friend, Michelle Blair—I am forever grateful for your brilliant insights, spiritually-grounded perspectives, editing opportunities, and our always enlightening "soul sister chats." To Valerie Jacobs — without her "rock star" smarts, creative collaboration and authentic feedback over the years, I could not imagine this book existing. To Yamilca

Rodriquez for inspiring me to go bigger. And to Johnna Craig, my biggest fan and supporter, I am blessed.

In more recent years, I am grateful to my Speed Art Museum family and the shared experiences of celebrating art together forever— I continue to be creatively-inspired. My Friday Girls Lunch group for the past 14 years— Colleen Beach, Tamar Schwartz, and Michal Kruger, I love that we still take the time for each other. And, my Girls Night Out group— Colleen Beach, Martha Slaughter, Patty Johnson, and Joanne O'Malley, our outings fill me up. You are each part of my tribe, thank you.

To my family, with immense honor and gratitude to: To Avery and Isabella who think I am the best Aunt, I thank you for your love and support. To my talented children, Taylor and Tess, who continue to brainstorm creative ideas and edit my work, I thank you for your unconditional love. To Elizabeth, I am glad you joined us on this journey and am grateful for you. To my stepdad, John, I am blessed by your faith. And finally, to my mom, Shirley— thank you for continuing to unconditionally believe in the importance of my work, and lovingly encourage my creativity. I love your strength, resiliency and support.

And most of all, to my amazing clients for sharing your hopes, dreams, wishes, fears, deepest desires and truest version of yourself with me— I am forever impacted by your courage, your vulnerability and the constant pursuit of your fabulous lives. Thank you for including me on your journey, allowing me to bear witness to your discoveries and for allowing me to compassionately learn from each of you.

# Introduction

Welcome to my second edition, *The True You Reimagined*. It has been almost nine years since I published my first edition, *The True You: Tools to Excavate, Explore, and Evolve*, and I am happy to be here again. When I published my original book, my intent was to compile the works that I had created for a local magazine and share the wisdom as I had created it in its original form as a marketing tool for my business, Excavive™ Coaching & Consulting.

My first book gave many people a chance to be inspired and motivated to be the best versions of themselves based on the premise of my Evolve column in *Underwired* Magazine. In it, I took my life coaching experiences coupled with insightful life lessons and then wrote a thought-provoking and action-inspired message based on the magazine's monthly theme. I am grateful for the opportunity to get my thoughts on paper and grow as a writer.

Almost a decade later, I revisited my work, and decided to reimagine it, resulting in the book you are now holding. *The True You Reimagined* is about being deeply connected to your core and staying grounded to live an inspired life. The root of who you are is strengthened and actively grown, while holding unlimited possibilities, dreams and desires. The book is now divided into six essential sections that assist the reader in revealing their true selves: Uncover Your Authenticity; Cultivate Balance & Being; Pursue Passion & Play; Enhance Your Work; Enrich Your Relationships and Break Free. I believe these six foremost areas are key to identifying what a fulfilling and authentic life looks like, as well as how to live it.

All of the chapters have been edited to reflect the wisdom I have acquired as a coach of 17 years. I deleted old material (that was hard!) and more importantly, added new material, including an entire Career section, to better reflect the needs of my audience. This evolution of my coaching work with the hundreds of clients who have been willing to include me on their path as well as the sum accumulation of my personal experiences brings a rich groundedness from the original format as well as freshly created, reimagined perspectives in the new work to best grow you.

My mission of serving others has not changed. It is my belief that if you uncover your essence—the deeper part of who you really are; define what is important to you; and then courageously take inspired action towards your dreams and desires, then you will evolve into the best version of you. You will be free to boldly explore all that life has to offer, breaking down any barriers along the way, and then live life with meaning, passion and purpose.

It is my hope that you will consider my "stake in the ground" opinions, incorporate the helpful lists and engage in the inquiring coaching questions and exercises. Part of *my* life purpose is to assist others in seeing their own beauty from within, excavating hope, inspiration and creative solutions along the way. I challenge you to form *your* opinions, as I am simply a provocateur for change, helping you to discover what's right for you.

Feel free to approach ***The True You Reimagined*** either from the beginning or focus on one section at a time. There is no right or wrong way to best utilize this book. It is simply a tool for discovery, transition and transformation. Anatole France said, "If the path be beautiful, let us not ask where it leads." Enjoy the journey, open your heart and soul and allow your world to expand by embracing love, passion and compassion along the way.

# UNCOVER
# YOUR AUTHENTICITY

**D**o you know who you really are and what's important to you? Do you live your life according to your values, fully expressing your true essence? If not, you are not alone. Many people go through life doing the things that they think they are supposed to do— I know, I did this for many years. I played a role doing what I thought I was supposed to do, trying my best to be a good wife, mother, community volunteer, daughter, sister and friend. But slowly, I left out an important part of that formula—ME. The truth is, I forgot who I was at my core.

Authenticity is described as the quality of being real, representing one's true nature or beliefs, being true to oneself; genuineness. For many people, they are able to be who they are in most areas of life. For others, they live a life according to the external influences that often override their own true needs. For me, I did show loving kindness and commitment to my family and causes but I also lost confidence in the freedom to be me— a passionate creative soul that needed to love deeply, express fully and make a deeper impact on the people whose lives I touched. I needed a spiritual connection and a better way to express beauty and creativity. When I divorced, I woke up.

As part of my journey and the self-work that I did, I discovered life coaching in 2003 and I felt like I had arrived. I came alive as I re-claimed who I was and in doing so, I realized that everyone is their best at their core. When one begins to peel back the layers of should's, challenges and limiting beliefs that are picked up along the way, then they can re-discover their value, worth and purpose. And from that place, the life one has always wanted can be created and sustained.

Uncovering your authenticity is a way to re-claim your essence, your power and your worth. Knowing who you are and what you have to contribute to the world is a beautiful progression, a journey not to be missed or wasted. Living your values each and every day allows you to make the choices that are empowering and sustainable to create a fulfilling life, as well as uplift the lives of others. Being authentic builds trust and sanctity, aligning your being with your doing in all of your endeavors.

I invite you to be open in the following chapters that touch on the ways in which you can discover what makes you, you. You will learn who you really are by defining your authentic values, exploring genuine ways to live your life, embracing the beautiful you, putting yourself first, being at home with yourself and mastering what life has to offer you. The world is waiting for the true you so let's get started uncovering your authenticity.

# Be Who You Are

*"By being yourself, you put something wonderful
in the world that was not there before."*
Edwin Elliot

Do you know who you really are, or do you hide behind a façade of selected masks and prescribed roles that have been handed to you by others? Do you reveal what is really important to you in the world, or simply shrink low when it is your turn to speak?

Society regularly asks us to fit in and to follow the norms, but does it void your vibrancy and suppress your spirit? If so, you are not alone.

Knowing who you are is important if you want to discover the full expression of yourself, and to experience deep love, personal freedom and true peace. On the outside looking in, most people look like they have it all together, and many do. Yet, they often believe something is missing... more fun, passion, authenticity, meaning, love, joy or full-out permission to be genuine.

Being real is essential to being truly happy, and it starts with claiming who you are and being willing to live that, day in and out. Aligning your internal and external worlds with your thoughts and actions creates a bona fide life. And, it will create sustainability in all that you pursue.

Living an authentic life is essential, but not always easy. It also requires a willingness to face fear, look deep inside and examine learned behaviors or bad habits and then transform them in order to move forward. It creates new ways of being in the world apart from your chosen roles, and that can take time and courage. Only then can you fully experience who you are… not only with others, but also with the most important person, you.

**12 Ways to Excavate Yourself:**

My "12 Ways to Excavate Yourself" are steps you can take to open the door and reveal your own authenticity. These areas will be explored more deeply throughout this book so let these initial twelve actions, along with a number of coaching questions, tips and exercises, assist you in evolving who you are as a person and designing how you want to reimagine your life.

1. **Live Your Values** Identify your values, what is important to you, and how you want to live in this world. Claim who you are, as opposed to letting others define you. Think about how you can live your life in alignment with your values.

2. **Embrace Beauty** People often say that beauty lies in the eye of the beholder. That means you get to hold the power over what you believe is beautiful to you, inside and out. Are you acquainted with what is gorgeous to YOU and what stirs your senses? Notice appealing sights, smells, textures, shapes, forms. Beauty is an inside job, so discover your own personal style and then let it reflect everywhere… in your clothes, home, music, art, nature, work you create.

3. **Pursue Passion** Know what makes you feel alive and consciously follow those activities that help you feel connected to yourself and others. Dance, sing, play, travel, dream, visualize, grow and create. Seek and expand your possibilities.

4. **Love What You Do** Are you following your bliss? Is your work irresistible, meaningful, or important to you? Engage in something you adore and brings you joy on a daily basis,

even if it looks messy or unexplainable to others. Be fierce for it.

5. **Be in Choice** You are always free to choose your thoughts, beliefs, attitudes and actions. Learn to say NO when you mean no, and yes when you mean YES. What do you choose in any given moment…heavy or light; easy or hard? Are you consciously making your choices with your thoughts, words, and actions?

6. **Practice Gratitude** Be thankful, understanding, kind, and compassionate; express it often. Let people know how much you appreciate them and what they do. Who and what are you grateful for? Start a Gratitude journal, say prayers of thanks, and acknowledge others' generous acts.

7. **Ask for What You Want** Do you know what you REALLY, REALLY, REALLY want? Practice wanting. If you ask for what you desire, you just might get it. Not asking is an automatic no. Communicate clearly and positively. And, besides, who knows what you want and need better than you?

8. **Trust Yourself** Trust your intuition. Your experiences will inform you, as well as your faith and wisdom to never go against yourself. Develop your self-confidence. Do you trust yourself? Upon whose opinion are you seeking or depending?

9. **Clear Clutter** What are you holding on to? People, places and things? Old memories, piles of stuff in your home or office? How are these "things" holding you captive? Keeping the unneeded holds an energy that will often hold you back, so clean it out *now*.

10. **Have Playmates** Are you spending time with people who honor you, celebrate you, or have similar interests, goals, values and vision? Engage in creative collaboration and amazing alliances. Who can you get to play with you on a project? Don't go it alone. Find people with whom you have fun personally & professionally. Enrich your circle of connection and enlarge your playgrounds.

11. **Try It Anyway** What holds you back? Is it a belief, an old story, low self-esteem or simply a bad habit? Risk changing. Be afraid. Do it anyway. A great idea without action is simply an idea, so do something new or different that moves you towards living your rich, authentic, rewarding life.

12. **Celebrate Success** When you reach your goals, do you stop to enjoy your fruits? Do you acknowledge your hard work, perseverance and determination? Rejoice and revel in all that you do and have done. Learn to savor. How will you celebrate, with whom and when?

## A Revealing Exercise to Help You Take the Mask Off and Be Your Best Self:

Take a blank piece of paper. On one side, write "MY PORTRAYED SELF" This is the person you show to the outside world, the many roles you play. On the other side, write "MY REAL SELF" and describe the qualities and values you believe you hold, in other words, your true essences.

Next, find a trusted person to share what you uncover about yourself–your secrets, fears, insecurities as well as dreams, desires and plans. Observe what is different on each side, and then brainstorm some ways to bring these two different sides into alignment. Create a final description of "MY AUTHENTIC SELF."

# The Authentic Wonder Woman

*"To thine own self be true."*
William Shakespeare

In thinking about women of today, I am amazed at how incredible women are. Women have businesses or careers, manage households, raise children, connect with romantic partners, work out and take care of themselves, spend time with friends, volunteer to worthwhile projects and organizations, indulge in hobbies, participate in book & supper clubs, save the world, attend church and Bible Studies, create art and music, go to social functions... all while trying to achieve balance, poise and grace. It is amazing they can play so many different roles and still have time to accomplish so much. Yet, I wonder, are they truly happy? Can they really do it all and maintain a life of balance and pleasure? And, are they being the truest version of their authentic selves?

On the outside looking in, most women look and act like they have it all together, and many do. Yet, my work as a Life Coach has shown me that something is often missing... more fun, more passion, more authenticity, more meaning, more love, more joy, full-out permission to be genuine. They are powerful and can be ambitious, yet real women rarely work on acquiring more things, making more money or obtaining more power for the sake of their egos and self-worth. They want their insides to match their outsides and to be fully transparent. The women of today long to maintain their personal power, use it for good in the world and at the same time be completely fulfilled and happy. They are the Authentic Wonder Women (AWW) of modern times.

In my Coaching business, I am hired by both men and women to help them rebalance and reprioritize their lives; re-discover who they are; and reclaim their own inner beauty, confidence, passion and self-worth. We create a partnership for re-learning of the self, and we engage in a very powerful process that is engaging, inspiring, accountable and forward moving.

To assist people in re-discovering their true selves, we start by defining a person's values, or the qualities that are most important to them. We excavate their inner depths, and then look at how well they are living their values in each of the basic areas of their lives. It is an opportunity to explore not only what is missing, but also see what's working. Some of the more common values we unearth are around adventure, freedom, beauty, belonging, creativity, helping or impacting others, connection, integrity, trust, fun, learning, love, passion, peace and harmony, and responsibility. The values are a "life checklist" and underlie everything they do. I always suggest laying a good foundation for your home before picking out wallpaper… this is what knowing your values does for you.

Once a client knows what is valuable to them, they can begin to make choices about what they do and how they do it, based on their own guiding principles. That is when the change begins to take place and we start to accomplish what has previously been thought of as impossible.

The AWW starts to feel more confident and acts accordingly. She feels more love for herself and others, and it shows. The AWW of today is the woman who is real in all of her many roles, and she makes the most of her life. She can balance the daily life demands while finding joy in whatever she is doing. It is always a choice, and she understands that. Ultimately, every man and woman I work with develop common traits that support their authenticity, as I have observed below.

## The Authentic Wonder Woman of today...

- **Knows her Passion and Purpose** She knows what is essential and why she is doing something. She pursues it with passion, cultivates creativity, infuses life with fun, and takes inspired action every day.

- **Connects to Herself and Others** She is all about tending to her important relationships. A quick phone call, a hug and kiss, making a date to spend time together, a simple "how are you?" She consistently connects to and loves herself, her tribe and new acquaintances.

- **Asks for What She Wants** She understands she is responsible for getting what she needs. She is boldly courageous in asking for it and speaking up by using her voice. She also knows when not to ask, as sometimes there is power in what she does not say.

- **Practices Gratitude** She is thankful for all she has and does. She honors her beliefs and those of others, and constantly recognizes how blessed her life is, even when there are bumps in the road.

- **Makes Mistakes** She recognizes the growth and learning in every misstep—mistakes are a transformational opportunity. She knows how to be responsible for herself, be vulnerable, doesn't take herself too seriously and laughs as much as possible.

- **Empowers and Helps Others** She inspires others by being who she really is. She willingly shares her gifts with others, reaches out to others and genuinely wants more for them than for herself.

- **Rejuvenates Herself** She feeds her soul. She prioritizes her time and gets grounded every day. She knows the importance of exercising, nourishing, sleeping, playing, meditating, praying, journaling, beautifying, spending time in nature, creating, having fun, reading, and halting... whatever nurtures her body, mind and spirit.

The Authentic Wonder Woman of our time is powerful beyond belief. When all women start to recognize their own magnificence, they will transform others as well. AWW can play many roles or choose various positions when desired. It only matters that they are being true to themselves and those around them while in those different roles. Females become a true Wonder Woman of today when they have mastered their own authenticity.

## Coaching Questions to Tap into Your Wonder Woman Within:

1. When was the last time you experienced true wonder?

2. What **unique** values, strengths or skills do you have that directly support your authenticity?

3. What distractions exist in your life that keep you from being your authentic self? List the things you do instead of being fabulous. (Yes, laundry can be included.)

4. What rituals do you engage in, or desire to create, that would give you permission to fully take care of yourself?

# Take a Chance on You

*"If you risk nothing, then you risk everything."*
Geena Davis

Taking chances in life is sometimes equated with a game to be played by taking risks, being careless or even reckless, or rolling the dice. Becoming successful is often a 50/50 probability of something working out the right way— based on the favor or dependency of others, being in the "right" place at the right time, having good luck, fate, or the generosity of the "Universe" or God, along with a good plan and lots of hard work. It takes struggling through, being brave, taking courageous steps and finally taking the leap.

Getting to the point of finally making a decision to move forward, much less take action, can be so hard. Yet, I believe it can be made easier by starting with YOU: what you deeply desire, what you believe in and doing your next right thing. What if taking a chance can be seen as an opportunity for full-on authenticity and permission to live in complete integrity by being who you are supposed to be and doing what you are meant to do, as opposed to basing your choices on the opinions of others? Ask yourself, "What do I want?"

Taking a chance on yourself is based on having a clear vision of what you want and embracing expansive opportunities, rather than reckless risks. It is about saying yes to you first— opening yourself up to the adventure of your life, thinking bigger, following the openings that are presented, being scared and doing it anyway. It is acting with clarity, self-confidence, faith and a knowingness of doing the right thing for the right reasons in spite of the fears that inevitably arise. When you take a genuine chance, you can ignite the feeling of freedom within yourself and reveal the opportunity to recreate and claim who you really are. Perhaps the "shortcut" to success is getting out of your own way, giving up the illusion of being in control, giving up what others think about you and letting go of fear as much as possible.

The process of Life Coaching is about moving you forward in any area of your life. From career and relationship changes to simply having more fun and creativity, my job as a Life Coach is to help you determine what you want and then look for what keeps you from actually being able to achieve your dreams. My clients are willing to take chances on themselves only after understanding what is important to them, creating a sense of balance, naming fears and then believing that they deserve to receive all the happiness and blessings in the world. You have to get out of your own way, face your fears and do it anyway. Only then can you take steps to move forward and take a real gamble on believing in yourself. Here are some thoughts on how to get out of your own way and let go.

## Take a Chance on Yourself by...

- being real
- deciding what would bring you the most joy
- getting out of the box
- creating a new life to go toward
- expressing your true feelings
- following your heart, not your head
- walking through your fears
- saying what you think and want
- letting go
- asking for help
- breaking a self-imposed rule when it no longer serves you
- acting on full faith

- practicing forgiveness
- experiencing and loving someone who seems unlikely
- releasing the outcomes
- trusting it will work out
- being wildly happy
- giving up the old for the new
- listening to your inner voice
- wanting more for others than for yourself (it comes back to you!)
- failing and starting over as many times as needed

Take a chance on you, your values, your abilities and not the opinions of others. Search your soul and do what feels right for you. Deeply trust that you will not betray yourself if you are in integrity with yourself, others and your faith. And always, always, always... follow your heart.

## Coaching Questions to Put You First:

1. What is the difference between being selfish and self-care?

2. Is your fear paralyzing you? If so, list *everything* that scares you and ask yourself if it is really true or not.

3. Start acting today based on who you want to be tomorrow... how can you be extraordinary now?

# Embrace Beauty, Inside and Out

*"Love of beauty is taste. The creation of beauty is art."*
Ralph Waldo Emerson

It is said that beauty lies in the eye of the beholder. Are you acquainted with what is beautiful to you? What stirs your senses, makes your heart beat faster and makes you smile? Do you know what makes beautiful people pretty?

Beauty can be defined as the pleasing appearance, impressive qualities and excellent aspects of someone or something. Many people are taught that looking at themselves and being concerned about physical attractiveness or a beautiful home can be shallow, selfish or in vain. However, I have always believed that taking the time to look and feel your best, as well as create beauty in everything you do, is a reflection of a strong self-esteem. Attractiveness is often focused on external appearances; yet it is equally important to cultivate your internal qualities and make it an inside job as well.

As a lover of beauty, I find that beauty must be experienced and reflected in as many aspects of life as possible. By taking the time to discover your own personal style, tastes and preferences, you can then let it emulate everywhere and in everything, especially in your looks, your surroundings, your activities, your relationships and your creations. Beauty in all its many forms must be witnessed, enhanced, preserved and shared. And what you create through your definition of beauty will be a mirror of your true essence and ultimately, an inspiration to others.

Beauty can be found everywhere in the ordinary and

extraordinary. It is up to you to open your eyes, mind, heart and soul to all that is present. Abraham Maslow said, "Some people have a wonderful capacity to appreciate again and again, freshly and naively, the basic goods of life with awe, pleasure, wonder and even ecstasy." Become a seeker of simple beauty, an explorer of magnificent wonders and searcher for all things good.

**Seven Ways to Experience Beauty in Your Life:**

1. **Source Inner Beauty**

   - Unleash your inner goddess
   - Develop a strong sense of self
   - Source beauty from within by being happy
   - Find gratitude, meaning and purpose in your work
   - Embrace full experiences and emotions through chaos and order, turmoil and calmness

2. **Reflect Outer Beauty**

   - Reflect what's on the inside
   - Create a healthy lifestyle to be your best
   - Find your personal style
   - Adorn yourself in fashion that looks good, feels good and enhances the true you
   - Finish your look with a smile

3. **Create Domestic Beauty**

   - Fill your surroundings with things you love, enjoy and appreciate
   - Bring nature indoors
   - Add colors to your palette
   - Clear as much clutter as possible
   - Have at least one beautiful room that is yours

4. **Invest in Relational Beauty**

- Nurture healthy relationships
- Enjoy simple pleasures with the people you love
- Be around positive people who make you feel good
- Learn about those you admire and why you are drawn to them
- Respect others and their uniqueness goodness
- Set boundaries when needed

5. **Embrace Organic Beauty**

- Strive to accept what is
- Go with the flow
- Make stillness part of your day
- Trust your intuition
- Make life effortless
- Worship the Creator
- Go outside and notice the beauty outdoors

6. **Discover Sensual Beauty**

- Know what makes you feel alive
- Pursue your passions
- Hold hands, kiss slowly and get plenty of physical touch
- Ignite your senses

7. **Allow Expansive Beauty:**

- Seek and expand interests and visual beauty beyond the mundane
- Visit art museums, listen to live music, watch the sun rise, gaze at the stars
- Marvel at something majestic

- Dream while you are awake

## Coaching Questions to Experience More Beauty:

1. How do you define beauty? What do you appreciate most about exquisiteness?

2. What is important, or not important, to you about your looks, your surroundings, your things or what you create?

3. Determine what lights you up from within. When do you feel most attractive? What are you doing, where and with whom?

Expand your range, richness and fullness. Canadian singer Kiesza said, "Beauty has so many forms, and I think the most beautiful thing is confidence and loving yourself." Embrace your beauty by adding more pleasing and impressive qualities to your life, inside and out.

# Don't Settle for Being Second

*"It's a funny thing about life. If you refuse to settle for anything less than the best, that's what it will give you."*
Somerset Maugham

I have been thinking about what it means to put yourself first versus putting the needs of others before your own. As a Coach, I often hear clients' concerns over appearing too needy or even selfish. I get it. It's important to be of service and consider other's needs as well as our own.

Yet, I also witness how people sacrifice themselves by not putting themselves in the mix. They take care of others' needs before their own and settle for being second. I propose putting oneself in the mix and truly embracing being first. Two is a great number for partnerships, but when it comes to having authentic, fulfilling relationships, how often do you or others you know settle for being the consolation prize?

People can accomplish much in many areas of their lives, yet when it comes to their relationships or their careers, they often resolve themselves or make compromises that do not honor what they truly need and desire. And, when the emotional stakes are at their highest, the bargaining begins.

Often stories get created such as someone, somehow, someday "it" will change and hope, coupled with denial, sets in. People hang on to promises made and they accept that their current career, life situation or relationship is as good as it gets. Even worse, some people do not even believe they deserve a better job, a wonderful relationship or the abundance that goes with a happy life. So, they settle for less without ever considering what they really need, much less speak up for it. This compromise often comes from a lower self-esteem or overcoming fear, thinking what one needs is not important.

Being first means knowing yourself, doing your best, believing you are worth it and asking for what you want. It starts with being clear about your needs, being proactive in achieving your dreams, and getting fierce for your desires. Making yourself a priority means asking people to assist you and if they are not able to, finding someone who can.

Insist on congruency with others in their words and actions and expect them to put you at the top of the list. Demand respect and start being treasured by the people closest to you for who you truly are, your gifts and talents and personal excellence. Create healthy boundaries when necessary and above all, get your needs met and be at the top of your own priority list.

## Identifying Your Needs:

Getting needs met can be a tricky thing. As humans, we have wants and desires, but often don't properly identify what's really missing or needed. In order to start living more authentically and joyfully, you must name it, claim it and take action. Consider what "needs" you currently have relationally, emotionally, spiritually, financially and physically. Listed below are the more prevalent needs I have observed in my coaching practice.

- To be valued, recognized, validated
- To be appreciated
- To be loved, cherished, adored, treasured, supported, approved of, acknowledged, cared for, accepted unconditionally, saved, rescued

- To be included, to belong, to feel part of
- To be liked
- To be certain, sure, confident, positive
- To be comfortable, nurtured
- To be free, independent, self-reliant
- To be noticed, remembered, seen
- To be of service, a leader, a follower
- To be trusted
- To be heard, listened to
- To feel important, needed, useful, busy
- To feel connected (to others, to a Higher Power, to yourself)
- To feel safe, secure, protected, stable
- To have beauty, order, consistency, perfection
- To have peace, calm, quiet, stillness, balance
- To have power, strength, influence, acclaim, control
- To have abundance, security, stability
- To have a cause, vocation, higher purpose
- To have honesty, sincerity, loyalty, authenticity, integrity
- To have fun, laughter, joy
- To have passion, play, pleasure
- To have companionship
- To have physical touch, connection

## An Exercise in Discovering How to Get Your Needs Met:

1. Using the above list, identify the three most important "needs" you currently want fulfilled, then rank them in order of importance to you.

2. Design three creative ways to meet each need.

3. Take responsibility to meet your own needs AND enlist four different people to meet each need for the next month—be sure to include yourself. Overdo it! Here are some examples:

- If you need to feel approval or validation, you might ask your boss for weekly check-in meetings or to tell you when you do a good job.
- If you need to feel adored, you might ask your partner to tell you how fabulous you are and maybe what qualities he or she likes about you.
- If you need to feel peaceful, you might schedule daily quiet time, start a meditation practice or go for a walk, without your phone.
- If you need to feel accomplished, you might make a list of your achievements you have done this year, so far.

# Be at Home

*"Everyone is a house with four rooms: physical, mental, emotional, spiritual. Unless we go into every room every day, even if only to keep it aired, we are not a complete person."*
Rumer Godden

Where do you live? I moved to Kentucky from Texas in 1990 and for many years, I still considered Texas my home. Even after I got divorced when my children were five and seven years old in 2002, I would still say, "I live in Louisville, but my home is in Fort Worth." When I chose to stay in my adopted state, I also decided to keep my children in their original physical home until they graduated from college.

I wanted them to have a happy, stable place to build memories as well as have their childhood house to return to in order to seek comfort, familiarity and love during their transitional years. I also wanted a large enough home for my Texas family to visit since I was a transplant. At the time, people told me I was crazy to keep my house, especially since I had no job, no income and few assets. So, I set off to do life on my terms and create my business— partly to make a difference in the world, but hugely to stay in my dwelling.

Fast forward many years later, my oldest child now has his own house and my youngest lives in a different city as of a few months ago. I officially completed the goal I had around my house when I got divorced almost 20 years ago. I also re-defined where home was for myself, as I finally embraced living in my adopted state.

As my family has transitioned, I am again thinking about my

home because it has served a huge role for me and my children the past two decades but now the people who have inhabited this space with me have moved away. I have also worked out of my home since I launched Excavive in 2004. So, I am pondering the many aspects of my physical spaces that make up a home, the real meaning of a home, and where I live, work and play.

For many people, home is defined by the boundaries of their physical space, or, their actual house. Others consider home to be their birthplace, their hometown or the house they grew up in. Several people deem their dwelling to be their current place of residence and the community in which they participate. Some people only feel at home when they are connected to a community; and they have created strong bonds with others by making new friends, getting involved as a citizen or volunteer, joining organizations, clubs and churches or synagogues, enjoying the natural landscapes, discovering the city's cultural opportunities such as the arts, sporting events and great restaurants, and doing meaningful work. And, finally, there are a few who believe they are residents of the world, finding that they are at home wherever they are in any given moment.

I am not sure how I will re-define my home in this life space, but I do know that it is time to expand my own definition of where I live and love. I have learned that home is as simple as where you belong and can be your full self, which can be your physical spaces, your family, your community and places that are sacred. So, where do you *live*? Where do you feel most at home? And if you are lost, exploring or wondering how you find your way back to a home base for yourself, here are some places to start looking and come home to.

**Five Aspects of Home to Consider:**

1. **The Physical Dwelling** Your house is the place where you live, your residence. It is the financial investment that is perhaps a mirror of your success and a pay-off your hard work. By caring for the actual home, keeping it clean and

clutter free, making improvements and designing it to your tastes, you create the headquarters for your life.

2. **A Reflection of Emotion & Beauty** Create a space that is reflective of you and your personal style. The colors, the textures, the scents, the lighting, the art, and the furnishings all set the tone and mood, and can provoke feelings of comfort, inspiration and joy. How do you want to feel in your space? What do you want to express? And, don't forget, the objects within that bring meaning, perhaps history, and allow for the further personalization of your space. William Morris said, "Have nothing in your house that you do not know to be useful or believe to be beautiful."

3. **A Container for Family** Your home is the place to create fond memories and build a rich archive for you, your family and friends. The daily routines, the milestone celebrations, the inevitable yet solvable disagreements, the actual caring of the home and its members, the playful moments, the sharing with friends and neighbors, and the safety and security of the house are all important aspects of building a strong home life. And, it can be a place your parents or other family members to visit or return to.

4. **A Community Playground** Have you experienced the feeling of coming home to familiar people and places by re-uniting with childhood friends or distant family, revisiting your old home or school, or dining at your old favorite standbys that still exist? Can you find connections to a new community by engaging in its cultural offerings, getting involved in a local cause or joining a church? Being grounded in a community allows you to find meaningful experiences and surround yourself with people who have similar values or interests. Being an island can be lonely but

finding a connected community can help you strengthen your home base and build a new, empowered sense of family and self.

5. **A Sacred Sanctuary for Self** And finally, home is always a place you feel content within yourself. Do you feel comfortable in your own skin? "I live in my house as I live inside my skin. I know more beautiful, more ample, sturdier and more picturesque skins; but it would seem to me unnatural to exchange them for mine," wrote Primo Levi, a Holocaust survivor and writer. To help you find inner peace, create a special space of your own within your home— a place to be quiet, a place to feel nurtured, a place to reflect, a place to breath, a place to feel your heart beat, a place to be your best, a place to be at home.

**Coaching Questions to Be at Home:**

1. Where is your home?

2. What qualities are important to you about your home... peace, comfort, safety and security? Beauty, family bonding, celebrations, entertaining, and community outreach? Security, business, financial investment, and success?

3. In what ways can you create a sacred sanctuary?

Johann Wolfgang Von Goethe said, "Be he a king or a peasant, he is happiest who finds peace at home." And, Sarah Ban Breathnach wrote, "Be grateful for the home you have, knowing that at this moment, all you have is all you need." So, whether you are a transplant to your current town, a homegrown city dweller or you have more than one house, you get to create your home to best reflect who you are based on your personal style, as well as to meet you and your family's needs. But most of all, don't forget that no matter where you are, home is wherever you are. Whether you are coming, going, staying, visiting, moving, shifting: YOUR best home is wherever YOU are.

# Excavate Your Best Self

*"We define ourselves by the best that is in us,*
*not the worst that has been done to us."*
Edward Lewis

My company, Excavive™ Coaching & Consulting was created in 2003 as a way to empower people, especially women, to pursue their passions, increase their self-confidence, communicate powerfully and build the kind of lives they truly want to live. The key messages I have embraced and promoted in my work have been rooted in evolving and uncovering one's authentic self.

Having worked with thousands of people over the years, I have come to realize that the core of someone does not change. But as people go through life, they sometimes forget who they are or get off track and then wake up and realize they are not living the life they really want. So, it becomes important to remember the core of who you are and grow yourself in the world as you go through life— anything from re-tooling past skills for a new job, re-igniting passionate pursuits, saying goodbye to people and places that no longer align, re-claiming lost relationships and pivoting to go in a new direction that may be better suited.

Being true to yourself is about re-claiming who you are by constantly being aware of your own values. Taking what life brings you, re-assessing along the way and then trusting yourself to make selective adjustments that still honor you is key to recycling yourself. Being authentic is the ability to reuse the good that exists from within you to make a discerning, positive impact on both yourself and others.

So, what follows are my most important messages and provocative coaching questions to inspire you. Knowing how to trust yourself by finding your own answers from within based on your deepest, soulful desires is one of the best ways to create an empowered and fulfilling life. Get started now by courageously giving yourself permission to be your best, no matter where your starting point exists and accept that life may need to be recycled along the way.

## The Five Most Important Messages to Evolve into Your Best:

1. **Empower Yourself First** Know your essence and what is important to you. Live your values. Reveal your inner self. Nourish and love yourself first. Take care of you so you can take care of others. Don't betray yourself and always be who you are.

   - Do you love who you are and how you show up in the world?
   - Are you living in a balanced way that is deeply satisfying and truly expresses you and your soul? (Be sure you live *your* life.)
   - Do you use your unique gifts to directly support your authenticity?

2. **Pursue Your Passions** Know what makes you feel alive and consciously follow activities that help you feel connected to yourself and others. Dance, sing, play, travel, dream, visualize, grow and create. Seek and expand your possibilities. Love being alive, know what you are passionate about, follow your urges, and be wildly happy as much as possible.

- What activities have heart and soul meaning for you?
- What does it feel like to be awed?
- What is your one unrelenting passion, and are you taking inspired action steps to manifest your reality?

3. **Communicate Powerfully** You are always free to choose your thoughts, beliefs, attitudes and actions so learn to express yourself authentically by communicating clearly, truthfully and positively; exuding confidence; creating connection; and listening actively. Do you know what you REALLY want? Practice wanting. If you ask for what you desire, you might just get it. Not asking is an automatic no. And, besides, who knows what you want better than you? Learn to say yes when you mean yes, no when you mean no. Make your words and actions meet. Set boundaries and say no often.

- Are you being nice or are you being real?
- In what ways are you using your voice to say what you mean and ask for what you want?
- Count the number of times you speak persuasively each and every day.

4. **Increase Self-Confidence** On a scale of 1-10 (best), how confident are you in your ability to have the life you truly want? In other words, what's your level of believability? It is important to feel good about yourself, the direction you are going and the confidence that you can do or have something. It's normal to be unsure, doubtful or scared, just don't let these things hold you back or doubt yourself. So, whatever it takes, fake it until you become it, and take the steps needed to be able to move forward knowing you can have what you want. Create a plan to increase your confidence by taking the next best step, every step of the way.

- Do you feel good about you?
- In what ways have you succeeded up to this point? Write a new story that includes all of the ways you are doing it right.
- How are you fully showing up?

5. **Build the Kind of Life You Truly Want** Create a life vision of what you want, now and going forward. Ask yourself if these items will create a sustainable "essence" of what you want long-term, i.e., greater intimacy with a partner, a more fulfilling career, creative inspiration for a passionate pursuit, slowing down, making a bigger impact or stronger connections with others. Are you following your deepest desires? Is your work irresistible, meaningful, or important to you? Engage in something that you adore and brings you joy, even if it looks messy or unexplainable to others. Create joy in all areas of your life and be fierce for it.

- What do you really, really, really want?
- How have you withheld yourself from life?
- Are you following your bliss?
- What could the best possible future look like?
- What distracts you? List the things you do instead of being fabulous.
- Do you live from the inside out or outside in?

Excavating yourself is about salvaging your goodness, accepting where you are right now and using all of your best qualities to move forward living an authentic life that is blissfully joyful, abundantly balanced, positively impactful and authentically meaningful. This is your great life, so make the most of it now.

# Life Mastery

*"One can have no smaller or greater*
*mastery than mastery of oneself."*
Leonardo da Vinci

I have lived a life half complete. As I look ahead to my October birthday each year, I reflect on the past six decades of my life. For some people, this juncture could bring on a melancholy mood after taking inventory of a half of a century's experiences. Yet for me, I am excited about my golden years of stepping into a truer, stronger, fearless and wiser me. I have always loved the end points of decades because I see it as an chance not only to create the next vision of what I would like to accomplish in a 10-year period but also determine how I want to step further into my own deeper, richer evolvement.

Looking back, I realize every decade has given me insights into myself, seeing how I have been both blessed and challenged. In my 20s, after college graduation I felt free and confident, maybe even conceited, to choose exciting experiences by traveling, loving my work and getting married. I was bold, brave, and fearless. Yet, I also suffered great loss with the murderous death of my father at the age of 23.

In my 30's, the successes of having children, a home, important community work and wonderful friends prevailed for many years, but sadly so did failures like my marriage and financial loss. I was humbled as I lost my faith, myself and the family life I had created. Up to that point in life, I did what I thought I was supposed to do, yet I also lost sight of who I truly was. I chose to divorce at the end of that decade.

In my 40's I re-awakened, remembering who I was, learning from all that life had brought me and became happy again. I re-built my self-esteem, created a new career and prioritized relationships. Every decade has brought the good, the bad and the ugly, and I continued to grow wiser as I got older and I learned to love the journey, understanding that every challenge became an opportunity to transform myself.

Being in my late 50's, I am continuing the work I started with confidence and clarity about the things I want, and don't want. I am enjoying life more, and honestly, am embracing all the wisdom I hope I have gained; and letting go of the things that I have no control over or no longer serve me. The Serenity Prayer by American Theologian Reinhold Niebuhr sums it up nicely— "God, grant me the serenity to accept the things I cannot change, the courage to change the things I can and the wisdom to know the difference." I am grounded and look for the joy every day.

As I continue on my path my next decade will be about life mastery, relaxing more into myself and using wisdom to stay on my journey and act accordingly in the world. I hope every gesture, thought, desire and action will be a reflection of my true essence. I want to inspire others with kindness, compassion, passion, forgiveness, vulnerability, creativity and love. I believe deeply in the power of one's personal path and the inner wisdom that can prevail when we take inventory and stop betraying ourselves, get out of fear, embrace our dreams, love richly and quit playing small in the world.

I want to live my bigger game in life by empowering people globally to live authentically. I also want to have richer relationships and simply enjoy life's pleasures along the way with ease and grace. My deep desire for others is that they will become ecstatically happy with themselves to live in their native genius and impact others positively. Too often, people overlook their goodness inside and out, and instead stay stuck, opt for the negative perspectives and meanwhile decades pass by.

The bottom-line is to learn your lessons and be true to you. Don't compromise who you are, what you want, and how you use your unique gifts. Because if you do, it might catch up to you someday in the form of regret, and the clean-up can be painfully messy. I recently came across an unattributed quote on wisdom that sums this up nicely: "Knowing others is intelligence; knowing yourself is true wisdom. Mastering others is strength; mastering yourself is true power." I hope you will be powerful, wonderful and wise.

## Jennifer's Life Manifesto:

Below is a sampling of the slogans I have accumulated over the past 20 years taken from many life lessons, teachings and inspirations. Put into an "Excavive Manifesto," these guidelines are intentions, opinions, objectives and motivations that have helped me to claim my beliefs, remind me to live fully and encourage others to do the same. I hope my personal platform will inspire you to create and claim your own wise wonderings.

- Uncover your authentic self.
- Be in BEAUTY.
- Find JOY in everyone and everything, every day.
- Cause no harm.
- Be of service.
- CREATE.
- Embrace your Brilliance.
- What's next?
- Speak your TRUTH; it is always good for you and the other.
- Live your values.
- Discover what makes you come ALIVE and do that as much as possible.
- Trust Yourself.

- Create your Army of Advocates.
- Date Yourself.
- Create your own definition of SUCCESS.
- Practice Gratitude.
- Pursue Passion, Play & Pleasure.
- You are always in choice, and you have the right to change your mind.
- You must have a space of your own.
- Go to the beach, often.
- Ask for what you want.
- Love what you do.
- Be scared and try it anyway.
- Embrace your "Succulent Wild Woman."
- Know that this too shall pass.
- Make conscious compassionate choices.
- Say YES by saying NO.
- Keep it simple.
- Pick 3.
- There is NO time to waste, get going.
- Clear out the clutter in your life so that new can come in.
- True connection cannot happen without the presence of vulnerability.
- Make no assumptions.
- Have do-overs.
- Practice forgiveness.
- Integrate intuition and wisdom.
- Have fearless fierceness.
- Exude vitality.
- All challenges are transformational opportunities to learn and grow.
- Celebrate and be celebrated.

## Create Your Own Personal Manifesto:

Using the above list as a sample, create your own personal reminders of your lessons learned, current beliefs, your own inspirations, and new thoughts for living. Here are some questions to guide you:

1.  What inspires you?

2.  What lessons have you learned that you wish you had known earlier in life?

3.  What reminders do you need to stay grounded?

4.  What dreams support the life you want?

# CULTIVATE BALANCE
# & BEING

A re you living a full life today? Do you feel alive and passionate about what you are doing? Do you know what you want more of in your life? If you answered no to any of these, your life might be out of balance and even worse, unfulfilled. And honestly, that's easy to do in today's fast paced world.

Many people seem to focus on getting up each and every day, doing what they are supposed to do, but it seems to me that many are just going through the motions. They talk about striving for work/life balance yet are still focusing on chasing success and waiting to live the rest of their life "someday." Someday they will take that vacation, date again, begin to exercise, spend more time at home, pursue their creativity, or take a chance on a dream. As a coach, I believe in radically prioritizing, consciously choosing and boldly making room for all the parts of life that need our attention on a consistent basis.

Balance can be defined as a state of emotional stability in which you are calm and able to make sound decisions. To be in equilibrium, to arrange, or adjust. Cultivating more balance and being in your life is about waking up and deciding how you live your life. It no longer allows one to just go through the day-to-day unconsciously, but rather provokes taking charge with knowing awareness. It's about being clear about who, what and when. It honors your journey and process; and gives you permission to have a fulfilling and joyful life now, not in some distant future.

I know— I used to live for my daily to do lists, crossing off the multitude of action items and feeling accomplished. I would dream about the bigger things I would do once I had more time or made more money. When I woke up to getting clear about my needs and desires, being fully present to my life and spending time with spiritual self as well as increasing my self-confidence, I began to discover ways to move forward in a beautifully balanced way and go after my dreams. My hope is that you will learn this too.

The following section will help you become in tune to what you really need in all life areas and how to start consciously making those choices. I offer you inspiration on balancing your life, taking inspired action, allocating your resources, moving forward faster, boosting belief in your dreams, managing stress, taking breaks, getting quiet, unplugging, developing your intuition and capturing your extraordinary moments. By cultivating balance and being, you will discover new ways to be peaceful, strong and happy as your truest self in the world, now and in the future.

# Balance Your Life

*"The greatest gift you will ever have is your life, and the second greatest gift - which you give yourself - is courage to live it to the fullest. Time goes by quickly, and you cannot take it for granted. Appreciate how far you have come and give yourself the gift of discovering how far you can yet go."*
Dr. Sonya Friedman

Do you have enough time to do the things you want? Are you always trying to manage your schedule so that you can squeeze a little more juice out of the few extra minutes and hours in a day? Do you feel like your schedule is driven by the demands of others, or worse, unrealistic expectations you hold for yourself? Does it ever feel like your sole focus is work?

If you answered yes to any of these questions, you might not have a balanced life. I am often sought after as a coach because people feel like they work too much and don't have time for the other parts of life. My clients are longing for more balance in their lives so that they can truly live out what's important to them.

There is much talk about work-life balance, and it seems to be a trendy topic. But I must admit, I do not like the language, work-life balance. I believe there is only life balance because work is only a part of how people should live their lives.

In the coaching world, life balance occurs by becoming aware of eight key areas of your life, determining your current level of satisfaction and then making choices to honor and prioritize each of these— career & education, money, health & wellness, friends &

family, romantic relationship, spirituality, fun & play and physical spaces. One area might take precedence over another at any given moment, but the point is to choose over and over again where to put time and energy into each of these.

Let's explore each area. But first, I ask you to answer the following questions: Are you living a full life today? Do you feel alive, passionate about what you are doing? What do you want more of in your life?

## Eight Life Areas to Balance:

1. **Career & Education** Why do you do what you do? Know your why. Do you love what you do? Are you receiving value, both monetary and recognition, for your efforts? Discover what makes you satisfied in your work and make sure the rewards match the job. If not, explore new possibilities.

2. **Money** Do you believe in abundance and that money is plentiful, or is tight and scarce? Does money come easily or does money evade you, causing you to doubt your own worth? What does money do for you?

3. **Health & Wellness** Does your body support your life? Do you listen to your body and act accordingly? Do you create the time to instill best practices for your longevity? This area covers sleep, nutrition, exercise, appearance, any medical issues as well as if you see your glass of life as half empty or full.

4. **Friends & Family** Savor your connections by giving as much as you receive. Let the people in your life sustain you and your dreams. Do your relationships build you up or tear you down? What boundaries or different choices do you

need to make? Are you spending time with the people you love and care about the most?

5. **Romantic Relationship** Melt away old relationships, resentments, patterns and bad habits in order to open your heart to soulful, romantic love. And, if you are single and want a partner, do you believe he or she really exists? If you are coupled, can your current relationship be re-ignited and fulfill you?

6. **Personal Growth, Spirituality & Religion** Let your faith and beliefs serve you on a daily basis. Give up the ones that hinder you or no longer align with who you have become.

7. **Fun & Play** Don't wait to instill play. Feed your soul by carving out time to play or learn something new. Choose your playmates and playgrounds carefully. Plan the big and small adventures. And don't wait for the "somedays." Life is short.

8. **Physical Spaces** Do you feel good in the spaces that you do your life— your home, your office, your car? What stuff needs to be thrown away, donated or sold in order to open up space for the things you want in your surroundings? If you do not love your physical backdrops, then what are you holding on to? Create a space that is reflective of you and you can call your own.

**A Coaching Exercise to Empower You:**

Take each section above and rate your level of current satisfaction, on a scale of 1-10, 10 being the highest level. Once you see your numbers, ask the following questions, and then think of small ways to support an integrated, balanced and interconnected life:

1. What is working, and not working, in my life?

2. What needs to be re-balanced or re-prioritized?

3. What immediate next steps could you take to create more life balance?

# Take Inspired Action

*"Your life will be no better than the plans you make
and the action you take. You are the architect
and builder of your own life, fortune, destiny."*
Alfred A. Montapert

So, you have some goals, a bucket list, a life vision or perhaps insight into an unbalanced life and want to make changes. You are excited about the future, yet you haven't quite started. Or, you might know what you want, but don't know where to begin. Another possibility is that you are just drifting along hoping things will get better. Wherever you are, taking action, big or small, can get you moving in the direction you want to go.

For most people, change happens through either inspiration or desperation. Many people get inspired to make positive changes with ease and grace, achieving their desired outcome with laser focus and few distractions. Some people begin their path but easily get off course and find it difficult to start again. And there are others who make excuses around waiting until they have more time, money, or energy or don't take any action until they are forced to. I get it—change can be scary, even paralyzing. It can be easy to get discouraged and do nothing. I find that people can easily lose faith, and often do not have the tools, supporters or clear vision to move past their fear. Until the pain of suffering outweighs the fear of the unknown, forward movement can't start to occur.

Whether you are restless, inspired, discouraged, challenged, excited, fearful or simply feel the need to begin again, why wait to take steps toward achieving your wishes? If you are ready to make a change in any area of your life, let's begin. The process of life coaching quickly moves people into action. I learned in my training from the Coaches Training Institute that there is a foundational belief that people are "creative, resourceful and whole and they have the answers within themselves," and this sets the tone for self-empowerment. My clients do not need to be "fixed," yet they often need to take bolder, more assertive steps to break bad habits, eliminate fears and create momentum. By tapping into integrated values, claiming realistic goals or intentions, and creating inspired action items, they gain the tools to have relentless courage and the self-confidence to have a great life.

It is important to have enthused deeds to turn a life vision into everyday reality so nice thoughts do not end up as simply beautiful dreams, a grown-up fairy tale or an on-going illusion. Even "hinting and hoping" (the way one wants something and wishes to get it without ever asking for it or doing something concrete about it) and "visualizing and manifesting" are not sole methods to making things happen. You must also take action derived from inspiration. So, use the positive energy created from hope, combine it with authentic goals and take inspired action to create everything you want for an enthusiastically blissful life.

When you begin to take specific steps towards what you want, you can synergize a cumulative effect on other areas of your life as well. For example, when you start working out, it makes you not only look good, but feel better. You then smile more, are at ease, are nicer and attract people who want to be with you. You then become more motivated in your work, do a better job, get a promotion or raise, etc.

Actor Bradley Whitford said, "Infuse your life with action. Don't wait for it to happen. Make it happen. Make your own future. Make your own hope. Make your own love. And whatever your beliefs, honor your creator, not by passively waiting for grace to come down

from upon high, but by doing what you can to make grace happen…
yourself, right now, right down here on Earth." Let's make it happen.

## Motivating Questions to Create Inspired Action:

In answering the following questions, you might consider how your
answers apply in the eight balanced life areas in the previous chapter.
Make a list of your answers and any related actions that inspire you.
Then most importantly, take action, any action, as long as you begin.

1. How far would you go to chase what you really want?

2. What's the next best step or low hanging fruit you could
   grab now?

3. Are you taking concrete steps to manifest your reality?

4. Have you begun today what you wish for tomorrow?

Envision a new beginning by expanding your hopes and dreams,
moving forward with inspired actions and embracing the rest of
your wonderful life. Drew Rozell said, "So I need to create a vision
of what I want that will bring all of my intentions together. And a
vision is just that– something I can see, something that's so exciting
and attractive to me that it pulls me forward until I have it." Begin
living your best life by taking action and discovering what awaits
you in the world.

# Allocate Your Resources

*"Life begets life. Energy creates energy. It is by spending oneself that one becomes rich."*
Sarah Bernhardt

Do you have a budget— a way to allot your resources for a given period of time? Does your plan line up with your inspired goals, authentic values, true desires and expansive dreams- or do you stay stuck in survival mode, just trying to make it and hoping it will all work out? When you hear the word "budget," do you get excited knowing you have a plan in place and feel positively confident that you make strong choices? Or, does the idea of a budget make you cringe with the negative thoughts of fear, guilt, doubt and uncertainty, making you feel like you are being held back, restricted or put in a box?

When people think about budgeting, they usually think about their money, or even their time. Discussions about how time and money are spent are everywhere, and for most people, it conjures up mixed reactions, good and bad. Many people are financially savvy yet might be challenged with how they manage their time. For example, they work hard and make plenty of money, yet they don't indulge in the things that bring them joy such as playtime, downtime, enough time with people they love or even fully using their vacation time. Others might be efficient with their time, and but lack the resources or the confidence to create more abundance in their relationship with money, and thus feel vulnerable in life.

It is important to consider how we direct our time and money to best utilize what we have. Yet, I think there's another area that is often overlooked, and that's our energy budget. Simply put- our energy is the life force in which we use to get things done. It's our stamina, power, intensity, vigor, vitality, our spirit. Energy is how we apply the resources we have. So, when we learn to protect, source and harness it, how we use our energy becomes critical to being able to truly maximize all of our resources.

An intentional budget of your time, money and energy commodities will serve the purpose of creating a foundation to best utilize all of your resources to live a rich life full of meaningful experiences and daily mastery. By getting your time and money handled easily, it will increase your vitality and free you up to do what is really needed as well as focus on what you truly want. It's the paradox of expansiveness- restricting what you have in order to better direct it and ultimately increase it. So, deliberately allocate not only your money and time, but also your energy. Here are some additional thoughts on purposefully directing your assets.

**Three Resources to Intentionally Budget:**

1.  **Money** What does money do for you? Money can provide security, stability, self-care, learning, adventure, philanthropy, validation, a solid future and a record of success. Your money choices can create either lasting satisfaction or instant gratification. Be in integrity, be generous and be smart with your currency. Although money is an exchange and measure of value, don't let money define your personal value or self-worth, but see it as an empowered energy to use wisely.

    •   What would you do with unlimited money?
    •   Does the way you spend your money align with your values?
    •   Do you include giving back and supporting your causes as part of your financial plan?

- What do you need to a financial clean-up— debts, overspending, planning, money leaks?
- Do you allocate dream money as part of your budget, allowing you to spend your money pursuing your goals?

2. **Time** Do you use your time wisely? It seems everyone complains about not having enough time, when in actuality, I believe it is how time is prioritized. Choose what is really important, be realistic and learn to break down greater endeavors into smaller increments. One way to think about time is to realize that every time you say yes to doing something, you are saying no to something else, and vice versa. Decide who and what you will say yes to and who and what you will say no to.

- What would you do with more time?
- Does the way you spend your time match your values and goals?
- Is your deadline real, or did you make it up? Are there other resources available so you can delegate?

3. **Energy** When you think about the many aspects of your life, energy is exerted for everything that you not only execute but also even think about doing. Mental, physical and even emotional exhaustion can set in if you are not being true to yourself. In order to get energized, it is important to identify who or what gives you energy, and who or what takes it away. By identifying the positive and negative influences, you can create more awareness of where the specific "leaks" exist; and then work to re-calibrate your vigor.

- Do you expend energy honoring your values and pursuing your passions?

- Do you protect your energy from the things that drain you, as well as invest in the people, places and things that give you energy?
- How can you double your vitality?

So, what's the point of it all? When you remove financial barriers, time limitations and energy drains, you can then channel your energy into moving forward and expanding your possibilities of fulfillment. As Author Terry McMillan said, "Too many of us are hung up on what we don't have, can't have, or won't ever have. We spend too much energy being down, when we could use that same energy - if not less of it - doing, or at least trying to do, some of the things we really want to do." Start by truthfully assessing where you really are, "right-sizing" your expectations, getting out of the "somedays," creating an intentional living plan, and then fiercely pursue all that you want and desire.

## A Coaching Exercise to Re-claim Your Resources and Direct Your Energy:

Using a blank piece of paper, create two columns of the following:

*A "Good" for YOU list*
    Who or what gives you energy; creates happiness and wellness; makes you come alive? List all of the people, places and things that bring you pleasure and add to your life. (Examples: friends, eating healthy, exercise, time off, massages, daily fresh air, fulfilling work, adventures, self-care, your assets)

*A "Bad" for YOU list*
    Who or what drains your energy? What are you tolerating? Who are your "energy vampires?" List everything that irritates you and is detrimental, big

and small, to your well-being. (ex: clutter, needy people, perfectionism, not using your voice, fear, skipping meals, your debts)

With the above information, begin to rid yourself (or set boundaries and limits) of the things that do not serve you. Identify the most draining energy zappers, and work to eliminate those first, while continuing to make time for the things that nurture you. Budget your energy towards increasing your abundance, your vitality and your overall life satisfaction.

# There is No Time to Waste: Get Going

*"We don't have an eternity to realize our dreams, only the time we are here."*
Susan Taylor

I am curious... have you done the things you have set out to do at this point in your life, or are you still living in the somedays? Are saying to yourself, someday I will take that amazing vacation, learn Italian, connect with old friends, do that home project, write a novel, clean out the basement, read a novel, explore a new hobby, get in shape or have a new romance? And, over time, do you find that your goals and to-do list start to look the same every year?

If so, you are not alone. As a Life Coach, I am hired to get people moving, but in that process, I often encounter people who procrastinate, are a victim of the "some days" or find themselves saying, "I'll get to it later," "I am too busy now" or, "After *this*, I will start *that*." Many people wait for the perfect partner, a different playmate, more money, the children to grow up, or the house to be clean. They think "I am the only one who can accomplish something, others can't do it without me or there is no one else to get 'xyz' done." Many of these people put things on hold indefinitely, make up excuses for not getting started and procrastinate, often causing unnecessary stress and constant disappointment.

I understand the need to balance life's demands and responsibilities. But I wonder why so many people don't get started sooner and become fiercer for their dreams? Even while visions are being created, strategies are being planned, motivation is being sought after and fear is being worked through, life continues to unfold and happen. Someone gets sick or goes away, a home repair costs more than expected or another project at work comes up.

Don't get me wrong, there are often legitimate reasons why the timing is not right to move forward on a project. And, waiting can be a benefit when it allows one to gather more information, build strength and confidence, adjust the vision or save more money in order to avoid debt.

But when days turn into weeks, months or even years, then perhaps it is time to make a courageous change, a daring move and decide to boldly move forward anyway. So, what is your heart's desire, and have you started making plans? Are you dreaming big and have you begun taking steps to make your life vision a reality? If not, what are you waiting for? Here are some ideas that might give you permission to get started faster.

**<u>Strategies for Moving Forward Faster:</u>**

- **Start with the big picture in mind.** What's the compelling reason to choose this?

- **Prioritize.** Create a "Life List" and make sure you ask yourself, "Is this what **I** want?"

- **Enjoy the journey.** Have fun along the way and attract he good things you want.

- **Use a Brain Dump.** Clear your mind and get out of the spinning in your head. Write everything down by thinking it and inking it.

- **Do the big thing first to get started**. Do something, do anything, just get going. You can adjust later.

- **Or, start with the low hanging fruit.** Sometimes starting small with more attainable successes will build confidence and momentum.

- **Create structure.** Clarifying attainable goals, becoming steadily disciplined and celebrating along the way will help.

- **Make expectations real.**

- **Be scared and try something anyway.** Face your fears and start.

- **Learn to say no to the unwanted and yes to what you really want.** Trust yourself and make sure you are doing your life, not someone else's. Don't forget to ask yourself, "Is this what I want?"

- **Be wholly present.** Do one task at a time and pay full attention in that moment.

- **Ask for help,** learn to delegate, enlist others or hire someone.

- **Be proactive instead of reactive.** Don't procrastinate and get ahead do the tasks you need to get done instead of reacting to the demands of others.

- **There is no good time and no bad time.** Prioritize pursuing your passions, anytime will do.

Get started, get going, just do something, anything, to move toward what you truly long for and desire. As Eleanor Roosevelt said, "Move boldly in the direction of your dreams."

It is up to you to embrace your dreams and not only wish for them, but to actively pursue making your world as big and wonderful as you want. Life continues to move forward, with or without you on board, and there are *always* good enough reasons not to do something and choose to wait. However, we do not know what tomorrow will bring, good or bad, so really, *there is no time to waste.* Tomorrow, it might be too late so, get going today.

## Coaching Questions to Get You Going:

1. What do you hugely desire to do, see or experience? What's going to ignite you and get you moving in a "got to have it" way?

2. Know the difference between a wish and a goal. Are your actions inspired by a compelling goal, or are they still hopeful wishes?

3. What excuses do you make? How do you limit yourself or hold back? Name your "stoppers." Refute them, prove them wrong and deny their hold on you.

4. Interpret your current situation powerfully and positively. Decide what you are going to do to "get going" and go do that now.

# Boost Your Believability

*"The future belongs to those who believe
in the beauty of their dreams."*
Eleanor Roosevelt

Here we go again… perhaps it is time to claim new year resolutions or set soulful goals, you've had another year around the sun; or are taking the opportunity to begin again with clearer intentions or a renewed possibility to really achieve all that you want in your life… you know, the really, really big stuff. A new career, a fit body, a big love, financial freedom, meaningful relationships, another home, or creative pursuits. I love the process of continually relaunching a life vision by checking in on what has been accomplished, asking the questions about where I am now, and then envisioning the future based on the continual growth and learning that happens as each year passes. I am inspired by imaginative actions that lead to marvelous joy, expansive vitality and stunning success.

Yet, as I write this, I wonder, why is it that some people can stay on a clear path of manifestation and stay true to the efforts to attain their dreams with balance and ease, and others can't? What does it ultimately take to remain focused and keep going toward one's aspirations when it sometimes seems unattainable, frustrating, too hard or flat out hopeless? What's the secret to the success that many people seem to have mastered, yet has completely evaded others? Is it luck and the stars finally aligning? Is it powering on with hard work and perseverance?

Those qualities can be part of the formula: claiming the vision, doing the work to back up the goal and sometimes allowing fate to play a part. But more importantly, I think the secret ingredient missing for many people is the importance of BELIEVING that you really can have what you want.

As a Life Coach, I am hired to assist my clients in achieving their goals in an authentic and sustainable way that honors them as well as the people around them. I instill clarity, confidence and passion, and hold my clients accountable to their wishes. Part of the process includes examining their belief system to see if their thoughts are empowering and moving them forward or are limiting and holding them back. If they are on track, usually they are taking steps to ensure their success. If not, their self-limitations of not deeply believing might be the problem.

Magic happens when you can source what you want from your own heart and soul, completely believe it exists, and accept nothing less for yourself than the best possible outcome. What beliefs do you hold to be true and positive? Prepare yourself to receive what you ask for, have faith it is on its way, continually relaunch as you gather new information and keep going each and every day, every step of the way. Here are some ways to instill a deeper belief that you can have what your heart and soul deeply desire.

### Suggested Ways to Increase Your Believability:

- Be clear about what you want.
- Envision the details.
- Use the power of words to claim your desires.
- Ink it and speak it.
- Have faith in God, the Universe, a Higher Power, or the Angels, enlist their help.
- Use prayer, affirmations, or intentions.
- Examine your beliefs- are they empowering or limiting?
- Launch your dreams.
- Go forward with self-assurance, confidence and certainty.

- Rid yourself of fear, doubt and ego.
- Be open to making adjustments along the way.
- Gather support from your caring collaborators.
- Banish the naysayers.
- Continue to transform, learn, and grow.
- Enjoy the journey.
- If you fail, begin again.
- Make yourself as happy as possible, in as many life areas as you can.
- Don't give up and don't stop believing, ever.

Henry David Thoreau wrote, "Go confidently in the direction of your dreams. Live the life you have imagined." Look into your heart and create an exquisite vision that honors you and the enchanting life you want, one that includes richness, fullness, passion and wisdom. Believe that you and your soul mate will find each other. Trust that the career you love will bring you abundance. Envision a healthy, fit and fabulous body. Imagine moving into your dream home. Believe you can publish a best-selling book. Create a new beginning that empowers you to believe that you will find something extraordinary, witnessing everyday miracles and embracing the reality of a beautiful, blissful life.

## Coaching Questions to Empower You:

1. If all things are possible, and you can have what you truly want, what would that be?

2. How certain are you that you can have it? Rate your believability on a scale of 1-10 (best) If you are below an 8-9, then consider what you need to deeply believe and look for evidence that validates your desires.

3. Where can you find magic in your life every day?

# De-Stress: Seek Serenity

*"Go in the direction of where your peace is coming from."*
C. Joybell C.

Do you take time to stop, assess and really think about where you are in your life? Do you give yourself the spaciousness to rest, ponder, think deeply and allow new thoughts to emerge? Or, are you always on the go or in a hurry, complaining that there is never enough time to get it all done, much less take time for yourself?

If this sounds like you, you might be stressed out. If you find that you take on more, want more, try to achieve more without understanding why— then perhaps taking a short sabbatical would be a wise investment.

I believe in striving for excellence in all that you do and creating big visions to pull you forward—but not when you sacrifice your self-care, physical body, spirit, innate creativity, relationships or peace of mind. It is important to take time off. After all, what's the hurry to get it all done now?

Seek serenity for the sake of better health and creating a clearer, more authentic picture of your life. You must go inward before you can manifest outward. If not, your vision might be blurry. It's like attempting to capture a gorgeous scene by taking a picture while the car is still moving. It can be fuzzy and out of focus. If you are always doing things on the fly, then you might be setting yourself up for more stress and its subsequent consequences.

I challenge you to intentionally hibernate in order to restore your body and soul. Search for inner wisdom during the stillness and then thoughtfully envision your next life steps. Proactively move towards what's next while instilling new healthy habits that you can use all year.

Actress Salma Hayek said, "People often say that 'beauty is in the eye of the beholder,' and I say that the most liberating thing about beauty is realizing that you are the beholder. This empowers us to find beauty in places where others have not dared to look, including inside ourselves." As you take time for yourself, learn how to de-stress, take extremely good care of yourself and use this state of dormancy to look deep within and discover what extraordinary qualities you possess that perhaps the world needs to experience through you.

## 20 Ideas for Creating More Peace & Serenity:

1. **Enrich you.** Put yourself first and take ultimate care of you. Listen to music, take long baths, get a massage, sing, putter, create new routines. You will be better for others if you are rested, replenished, nourished, and happy.

2. **Create your life vision.** Plan something to look forward to that is meaningful and purposeful. Daydream often. Set soulful goals.

3. **Embrace life balance.** Balance is not work/life only... it includes career, money, health & wellness, friends & family, romantic love, spirituality, fun & play and physical spaces. EVERY area needs attention and is of equal importance.

4. **Plan your time.** Slow down and "right size" your schedule. Use 15 minutes daily to decide what you really need to do. Discern what needs to get accomplished now or can wait until later. Ask yourself, "How important is it?"

5. **Connect daily with people you love.** Don't miss the opportunity to show how much you care. Be a friend.

6. **Pursue your passions**. Ignite your inner fabulousness, come alive, and make time for the activities you love.

7. **Get active**. Move, exercise, dance, go outside regularly; don't live a sedentary life.

8. **Be joyfully present.** Focus on your current task or experience in that moment. Don't multi-task and be completely engaged in what you are doing. Express your joys freely.

9. **Behold beauty.** Open your eyes to the magnificence around you, both yours and others. Watch a sunrise or sunset.

10. **Say NO often**. Set boundaries and don't go against yourself. Stress is created when you are not true to you.

11. **Ask for help**. Speak up for what you need and want from your support system. Build your army of advocates and tell them what you need. People don't know unless you ask.

12. **Take time daily to be quiet.** Relax and get out of the hurriedness of life. Meditate, pray, read, do nothing, take a nap, see the good in life and yourself. Create traditions and rituals. And, breathe.

13. **Be proactive rather than reactive.** Keep it simple, keep your side of the street clean. If something needs to be tackled, just do it now or take it off your list. Stop worrying.

14. **Remove negativity from your life.** This includes people who make you feel bad, watching the news, having negative thoughts, participating in gossip or seeing clutter in your spaces.

15. **Laugh often.** Find your sense of humor and keep things light. Smile.

16. **Have gratitude every day.** Who and what are you thankful for in this moment? Count your blessings. Give to others and do something unexpectedly for others.

17. **Write, journal, make lists.** Get out of your head and let your thoughts flow freely. Do a brain dump, if needed.

18. **Take inspired actions.** Do something toward your dreams will bring a sense of peace, even if it's a small step. No action causes stress. Will "this" action move you closer to your dreams or away from them?

19. **Increase your emotional intelligence.** Recognize your feelings and express them appropriately. Use anger as a motivation for change. Increase your EQ.

20. **Celebrate your successes.** Build in rewards along the way. Recognize an achievement, be proud.

**<u>Coaching Questions to Consider:</u>**

Create a place to retreat and rest. Settle into your favorite spot, make a soothing drink, gather your journal and any other reading materials. Once you are cozy and comfortable, define what "down time" means to you.

1. What will replenish and re-charge you?

2. What boundaries do you need to create?

3. What does ultimate nesting and rejuvenation look like going forward?

# Take a Break: Plan Your Next Adventure

*"The biggest adventure you can take is
to live the life of your dreams."*
Oprah Winfrey

When is the last time you really got away? Where have you been lately that has allowed you to mentally leave your work behind, enjoy time off, relax, create a new memory and really do what you want? During the summer months, there seems to be more opportunity to think about vacations, breaks, pauses, immersions and escaping with children out of school and the hurried pace of activities slowing down. Holidays also creates natural time off, yet there is so much busyness that they rarely feel restful.

So, when is the best time to get away? What purpose do breaks serve? And, do we really know how to get away?

There is no doubt that taking breaks can nurture the body, mind and soul. Our society supports time off in many different forms such as coffee breaks, weekend getaways, the traditional two to three weeks of vacation time and sabbaticals. People have become better at getting out of the daily and weekly grind by engaging in activities that fill up their tanks. Meditating, working out, reading books, being outside, daydreaming, seeing movies, socializing, lunching and "dinnering," being alone, creating technology-free zones, planning spa days, taking bubble baths, going on short getaways… these are some of the respites that keep us going.

Yet, I wonder if these smaller activities are enough to truly sustain us? Are we taking the longer breaks that allow us to completely unwind and give us joy, fun, adventure and learning? When it comes to long-term health and happiness, are we balancing the leisure interests, hobbies and grounding tools with the peak experiences and big adventures that produce greater fulfillment?

I am as guilty as everyone else about taking time off. I work hard, love what I do, and I am pretty good about maintaining balance, having solitude, engaging spontaneity and vacationing with family and friends. I work for myself, so I can get in the habit of going through the motions of time off but not truly take a break from my work.

When I finally learned to stop for a ski holiday a few years ago, I set aside everything Excavive and was able to fully enjoy my trip by skiing, nurturing my relationships, reading a historical fiction book, drinking wine by the fire and resting. When I returned, I re-prioritized my work balance and was able to gain the personal and professional growth I had been seeking. Now, I regularly plan big escapes, and I invite you to think about your getaways as well.

## With the Busyness of Life, Why Stop and Take a Bigger Time Out?

- to get away from the mundane and routine
- to create self-awareness by noticing who you have become
- to find new inspiration and creativity
- to see beauty in your surroundings and situation
- to remember why you made the choices you did
- to avoid burnout
- to check in and see if yesterday's goals still fit tomorrow's dreams
- to connect with the people you treasure
- to tap into your intuition
- to have fun

- to learn something new
- to rejuvenate, relax and breathe a little easier
- to get clear about difficult or challenging situations
- to create a more colorful archive of your life

From spiritual practices to carnal pleasures, I have learned that the everyday habits and positive endeavors support us in creating balance, connection, productivity and grounding. The short retreats, whether they are healthy diversions or dreamy virtual experiences, give us a sense of freedom, re-charge the batteries and are fun. Yet, the bigger adventures help us in reaching our pinnacle. Decide what you want to do daily, weekly, monthly and annually. Replace "someday" with today and start planning an aspiring adventure of a lifetime.

## A Coaching Process to Create Your Life Adventure:

1. Make a list of things from which you need a break.

2. Now create a list of things you are longing to do.

3. Decide how much time you need for each one… an hour, a day, a week or longer? And make a plan.

# Unplug

*"Some people have a wonderful capacity to appreciate again and again, freshly and naively, the basic goods of life, with awe, pleasure, wonder, and even ecstasy."*
Abraham H. Maslow

When I started thinking about the topic of unplugging, I realized how much noise and discussion currently exists about the need for this, yet I wonder how many people truly allow themselves to be lazy?

People spend a good deal of time doing, and very little time relaxing, stopping or simply being. In a fast-paced, achievement-driven society, the people who get ahead are those who are diligent, hard-working and energetic; not those who are idle, sluggish, slothful or resistant to exertion. However, in all of the daily frenzy of a modern life, people are not only mentally unfocused and physically exhausted, but also have forgotten why they are doing so much running around in the first place.

I believe that in order to be truly happy and successful, you must learn to unplug and create a more rhythmic life that balances what we do with resting the body, mind and spirit. In other words, being lazy is essential.

Sounds simple, but how do you really reduce your speed? First, be aware of the signs indicating a respite is needed. Recurring or obsessive thoughts, being stuck on a problem that's not getting resolved, experiencing creative blocks, scheduling or planning every moment, lacking in joy, getting physically sick or run down, or feeling depressed and lethargic are all indicators that you need to slow down.

Second, be aware of the reasons keeping you from taking time off. Get rid of the silly excuses, fears, and unrealistic expectations; and make a stand to take care of yourself first. And finally, begin to replace old patterns with new ways of unplugging. Since everyone needs something different, listed below are some specific suggestions that can be implemented in small or big ways.

## Ten Ways to Unplug:

1. **Mentally** Take a break from your desk, computer and telephone and be "unreachable" for 15-20 minutes. Walk outside, read something for fun, or go to a coffee shop. If you don't already do this, go out for lunch. Create scheduled time off to take a break from your normal day to day musings. And, always use all of your vacation time, even if you stay home and do nothing.

2. **Financially** Give yourself a break from constantly watching the stock market or your bank account balances if it creates stress for you. Instead of checking your accounts daily or weekly, check in less or hire an advisor. Create a reserve and set aside "fun" money. If you do the bill paying, ask your spouse to take turns with you.

3. **Physically** Make your movements slow and deliberate; saunter instead of rushing. Integrate slower activities such as yoga or walking. Engage in nurturing activities such as baths or massages. Eat in silence and savor every bite. Turn off the alarm clock, especially on the weekends.

4. **Relationally** Take time off from being the planner, organizer or hostess by allowing others to take the lead.

Set boundaries, when needed. Schedule a "Pajama Day" or other forms of being lazy at home. Take time to be by yourself.

5. **Emotionally** Understand how you feel, what drains or exhausts you and what you need to do to step away and be introspective. Give yourself the needed breaks to internally re-group.

6. **Romantically** Let go of old resentments and bad habits. Take a break from "nit-picking" and overlook your mate's shortcomings, even if it's just for a day. Make a date by staying in and inviting your partner to be lazy with you. Create a soft place to land with your partner and relish in the love and support.

7. **Spiritually** Cultivate an inner laziness to create peace and calm. Stop fretting and worrying. Let yourself fall asleep when you are tired. Enact the Sabbath as a day of rest. Trust God, your Higher Power, or the Universe. Be comfortable with and ask for alone time. Journal. Pray. Meditate. Be in the moment. Daydream.

8. **Socially** Plan nothing and see what you feel like doing; follow your energy. Choose low-maintenance playmates. Select activities that require you to slow down: float in a pool, take a blanket to the park, lie in a hammock, spend time in nature, get lost in a romantic novel, watch movies in bed, play board games, read poetry or listen to classical music.

9. **Technologically** Create technology-free zones daily and weekly. Turn off your devices and take a break from the screens and pings that constantly want your attention. Read

a book or take a walk outside without being connected to your phone, computer or iPad.

10. **Structurally** Take a day off from chores and let your house get messy for a few days. Hire a housekeeper. Simplify, de-clutter and create comfortable places to relax in your home.

In his book *Sabbath*, Wayne Muller writes, "Sabbath is a way of being in time where we remember who we are, remember what we know and taste the gifts of spirit and eternity." By being lazy, you can get re-energized for the necessary work and create space to honor a period of rest that will restore you to your essential greatness.

**An Exercise that Gives You Permission to Halt:**

1. From the above list, choose three areas to renew yourself. Determine your *easiest* ways to rest and rejuvenate.

2. Ask yourself, "when I get to the end of the day, how do I want to feel?" Schedule relaxed, carefree, lazy and unstructured time off. Refine your daily, weekly and monthly rituals.

3. Give yourself permission to slow down. You can use my Excavive "Permission Slip" in the Appendix.

# Awaken the Small Voice Within

You may have heard of ESP, intuition or even someone's psychic abilities to provide answers to the unknown, or even make predictions about what is happening in the past, present or future. Do you ever wonder if that sixth sense is valid? And if so, who has it, where does it come from, how is it used and why is it important?

In my opinion, developing your intuition is one of the greatest gifts you can give yourself. When I chose to become a coach in 2003, I had already been on an awakened spiritual path for several years. So, as part of my preparation, I decided to participate in "Intuition" training in Sedona, Arizona. I learned that getting quiet on a daily basis through meditation and journaling was key to listening actively. But more importantly, since then, I have learned that seeking wisdom in silence; fully trusting myself; improving my faith; leading a clearer and more peaceful life as opposed to being in chaos; being proactive rather than be reactive to people and situations; and believing in my abilities are supported by my intuitive resourcefulness.

Yes, I sought out a special training, but the truth is, I believe everyone has the ability to tap into their own deepest knowing and to listen to that small voice inside. This powerful intuition is an inner knowing; recognizing a sign or observation that brings forth a truth before it is revealed to the outside world. It is a gut feeling supported by faith, a place of peace, a sense of harmony, and an all-knowing trust that all will be well.

Many people believe their initial five senses tell them everything they need to know. However, having a keen perception of what you see, hear, touch, taste, and smell externally is not enough to fully discern the conflicting messages that are often present. Sometimes there are random coincidences, such as when you think of someone and they call, or when a book falls off a shelf and you think it is a sign to purchase it. Be judicious by going inside, stay on purpose and learn to find the answers within. Become more empowered by deciding what is true and right for you.

So how do you access your intuitiveness? It starts with learning how to be still, developing a consistent meditative practice, committing to a quiet time, journaling, paying attention to your gut feelings, and listening to your intuition. Be intentional about making time for reflection by scheduling white spaces on your calendar. Give yourself enough time to think, daydream, ponder, read, and write—all without speaking or being spoken to. Become conscious and aware. And protect any negativity that can easily seep in.

Design your perfect surroundings. Find a place of your own where you feel safe, peaceful, authentic and grounded. Deliberately design that place to be still— perhaps it is a special room, a comfortable chair or even a spot outside where you can take a blanket or your yoga mat. Also, be open to the fact that God speaks through others, both the likely and unlikely. Observe your successful hits and learn from the times you ignore the internal warnings. Practice awareness and trust that time will build a strong inner compass. By accessing your insights, you can create more consciousness, creativity and aliveness in your life.

**Six Benefits from Developing Your Sixth Sense:**

1. **A Strong Sense of Personal Self** and the ability to be more confident, self-assured and grounded. This is where self-trust develops so that when you hear that small voice, you can follow it with conviction and ease. Self-betrayal will cease to exist, and healthier relationships will emerge.

2. **A Sense of Responsibility** by helping to determine what is right and wrong. By stopping long enough to ask yourself your truth, you can strengthen your own moral code and be more responsive to others. In other words, if you pause, you will do the right thing for yourself and others.

3. **Compassion and Empathy for Others.** This is about having acceptance and being of service to others by teaching, bringing comfort, healing and caring for the members of your community so that everyone can benefit. This breaks down the ego, helps navigate what the other person needs and allows you to walk in another's shoes. By seeing the good in others and yourself, a more loving connection can occur.

4. **A Sense of Justice** can prevail. Being aware of balance, fairness, and seeing other's perspectives while maintaining your own integrity can equalize any injustices.

5. **Inspiration and Creativity.** The ability to express passion, connection, love and any other messages through your artistic talents can surface when your sixth sense is present. I know when I am writing, some of my best ideas emerge when I have solitude by napping, being still and getting as quiet as possible. Walking in nature also helps.

6. **A Healthier Body.** By reducing internal chaos and quieting the gremlins in your head, you can reduce the stress that contributes to "dis-ease" and physical ailments. Listen to your gut, as the body always knows when something is not right before our conscious mind is tuned in. And, a healthier you promotes clearer thinking, harmonious living, beauty and a more peaceful existence.

Align your heart, mind, body and soul by listening to what is revealed about the poetry of your life. American actor Alan Alda said, "You have to leave the city of your comfort and go into the wilderness of your intuition. What you'll discover will be wonderful. What you'll discover is yourself."

## Coaching Questions to Help Access Your Sixth Sense:

1. What is it to be insightful?

2. When you want blissful solitude, where do you find your uninterrupted escapes that allow you to listen and be peaceful?

3. Under what circumstances are you able to "receive" internal messages through your intuition? Do you listen to or ignore them?

4. How has your intuition been validated? Make a list of all of the ways you have learned to trust yourself based on following your instincts.

# PURSUE PASSION & PLAY

D o you have a passion-filled life? Are you having fun, every single day? Are you engaging in the things you love— at work, at home, with the people you love, in a place where you feel like you belong? What do you create, and why? What makes you angry in the world; or come alive so much so that you can't not do something about it?

These are some of the questions I ask myself and others when pursuing passion and play on a consistent basis. What is it to be fully alive doing what you love? To me, excavating your deepest passions are extremely important. It's what keeps me engaged and feeling connected to myself, to God, to others, and to the causes I believe in. It supports my creativity and aides in being inspired. And the risk of not fully expressing myself in an authentic way can lead to the slow death of my soul. I know, I was there at one time.

Passion can be defined as a strong or extravagant fondness, enthusiasm, or desire for anything. At its best, it's a powerful or compelling emotion that evokes action. So, to actively follow your aspirations is one of the best ways to be authentic and make a powerful impact in the world. Plus, it's a lot more fun along the way.

For me, my passion shows up in my work when I am writing, coaching or delivering a speech. In fact, in my earlier days of Excavive, I used to take a salsa dance lesson a few hours before a speaking event because the flow of movement connected me to my body and myself. The swelling up of feeling grounded coupled with the flow of dancing opened up a channel for whatever I had to say in that moment. Now, other playful activities such as Pilates, yoga, listening to music, cooking, walking in nature, putting together beautiful outfits, traveling on art trips, exploring new places, attending concerts, making love and arranging flowers continue to inspire me and make me present to my life. In fact, some of my best ideas come to me when I am at play.

Pursuing passion and play is important because it's what keeps you alive, fuels the desire to keep going and results in true pleasure. And, when you pursue your deep desires, you are living your true self. This section will assist you in becoming more playful, more sensual and freer to be you. There are chapters on igniting your passion, having fun, discovering what's possible, excavating your creativity, tapping into your power, connecting to your sexual self and creating your personal passion guidelines. Enjoy the rapture of discovering your truest passionate you.

# Ignite Your Inner Passion

*"What is passion? Passion is surely the becoming of a person."*
John Boorman

Do you feel alive and present in your life? Are you doing the things you love in your work, in your home, in your community and your relationships? Are you raising your heart rate on a daily basis, whether you are exercising or making love? Do you have a passion-filled life?

Sometimes when I speak to audiences about passion, people first think of sex or the things they will do some day when they have more time or money. Passion is secondary for many people and so they settle for observing it in books, movies and the lives of others, rather than embracing their own wants, needs and desires. The truth is—passion is a powerful feeling, a deep connection, a strong longing for something or someone, and I believe it needs to be awake in as many parts of your life as possible.

Passion is the beginning of a dream or an idea. It is the fire burning inside you when you feel completely aligned with your thoughts, feelings, desires and values. Pursuing fervor makes you vulnerable and encourages you to have ecstatic experiences to give you the confidence and knowingness to start a new path and get what you want. Rebecca West said, "It is the soul's duty to be loyal to its own desires. It must abandon itself to its master passion." Passion can be described as a spontaneous act of abandoning all reason and that is exactly what you need to do. Get out of your head, listen to the longing in your heart and intentionally move forward even when it may appear to be irrational, unreasonable and downright crazy to others or even yourself.

Excavating your deepest passions are important. You must find ways to outwardly and concretely unleash the suppressed desires that align with who you are and what impact you want to have. The risk of not expressing your essence is the shriveling up of your soul, a slow death in your relationships from the lack of love and isolation, a deficiency in enthusiasm leading to the waste of your unique talents, a possibility of creating emotional and financial poverty, living with faded dreams and unfilled hopes, and the separation of your spirit from God or your Higher Power.

Passion is everywhere, in everything and reflected in everyone. Open your eyes to the passion surrounding you, let it envelope your existence and then tap into your inner knowing of what turns you on. All great ideas start with dedicated excitement, and you must practice fearless fierceness for a passion-filled life. Here are some ideas to turn on your personal passions.

## **Ways to Turn on Your Passion:**

- Be fully present to what you are doing and completely engage with those around you.
- Get out of your head, pay attention to your heart's desires and trust your gut feelings.
- Do things that make you feel good.
- Let your inner beauty be reflected in your outward appearance in your clothes, jewels, hair and make-up.
- Only buy things that you love and have the experiences you want, no "should" allowed.
- Achieve your personal best body for you and no one else.
- Tap into the five senses of smell, taste, sight, hearing and feeling to create your own sensuality.

- Look for your partner's soul through his/her eyes. Let him/ her take your breath away and feel your heart race.
- Make love... A LOT.
- Spend time with people you want to be with, not people you have to–and really get to know them.
- Add romance, magic and sparkle into everything you touch.
- Liberate your physical spaces by cleaning out clutter, bringing in beautiful items and adding colors that inspire whatever emotion you want to feel.
- Go outside and look at the stars.
- Be fierce about your creative pursuits.
- Take time for cultural experiences like concerts, art exhibits, lectures, reading, opera, ballet and traveling so that you can be inspired.
- Dig in a garden.
- Play with your children.
- Be spontaneous by following your urges.
- Engage in rituals that make you feel grounded and connected—prayer, meditation, church, journaling, quiet time, lighting candles and listening to music.
- Eat dark chocolate and drink fine champagne, or anything else in which you take delight.
- Dance when you are alone.
- Focus on fun, laugh a lot and don't take things too seriously.
- Savor the climatic moments of your life.
- Don't waste another moment... get started now.

When you fill your life with divinely inspired acts and are actively engaged with things you truly love, then your life will transcend and fall into place. Your spiritual, mental, emotional, physical and creative pursuits will attract the perfect partner, the dream job, deep faith, a healthy body, the abundant bank account, the completed novel, true friendships and a beautiful home. By playing with possibilities, dreaming about new ventures, meeting zealous people, making a difference for others, and seeing the world from new perspectives, you bring passion not only to your life but also to those around you. Passion is contagious and available everywhere, in everything and for everyone at any given moment. Ignite your inner passion today.

## A Coaching Exercise to Discover, Ignite and Expand Your Personal Passion:

1. By answering the following questions, create a list of the things you are passionate about:

   - What activities energize or intoxicate you, get your heart beating faster, take your breath away and make you come alive?

   - What makes you hot and bothered? It might give you some clues as to what you truly care about.

   - If making love is bringing love into the world, what can you do to bring more love into the world?

2. Choose the activities that you are most excited about, prioritize these and start at least one new passion-filled pursuit today.

# Frolic, Fun and Play... Every Day

*"The world is your playground. Why aren't you playing?"*
Ellie Katz

Are you having fun? I mean, really seeking pleasure consistently, not just the lighter and brighter months. For instance, summer is a time that is relaxed, carefree, lazy and unstructured. It is the perfect time to frolic and play and have fun every single day. School is out. The pool is open. Trips are taken. Movies are watched. Books are read. Lemonade stands pop up. Gardens are tended. Parks are filled with people playing sports, taking walks, riding bikes or listening to concerts. Families reunite. It is a time for celebrating, being in the moment and taking breaks from the routine of our lives.

Frolic is defined as playful behavior or action, merriment, gaiety, fun... so how much fun are you *really* having? Are you taking time to build play into your life, every day, all year? People often wait until the warmer months to indulge, but you can start now, because why wait until a specific season to enjoy your life? Why not find the fun in every season? For example, I love the Fall because it's the beginning of the Arts season filled with art openings, the Orchestra, the Ballet and the Opera. Winter is a time for more inward fun such as reading by the fire, learning something new, time with family and snow skiing. And of course, Spring brings a renewed spirit of celebration because after all, it is Derby time in Kentucky.

In my Coaching practice, I have observed how difficult it can be for people to take time off. People from across the nation come to me for various reasons: some are seeking answers regarding their careers, making more money, setting new goals, or finding the right person. And even though these desired changes are important, I often learn that the key missing element in their lives is not having enough frolic, fun and play... not the better job or different relationship. When we add more fun into their lives, their careers and relationships often improve.

And, the truth is when you focus on play and enjoyment you can create more overall happiness in your life and achieve your goals faster and easier. Your joy will become a magnet for the things you actually want in your life. So, what keeps people from having fun? My clients tell me their reasons for not delving into their true passions are because: "I don't have enough time;" "I don't have enough money;" "I don't have anyone to do that with;" or "I will do that *someday*." I believe these are just excuses and stories. I say to them, "If not this, what?" and "If not now, when?" It's time you have more of what you want by creating more playful opportunities each and every day. Here are some ideas to get you started.

## Nine Ideas for Infusing More Fun in Your Life:

1. **Love Being Alive** Savor your experiences and choose joy each and every day. I wake up every morning and start the day off by saying "I am so happy and grateful for ____."

2. **Play with Passions** I love travel, yoga, Pilates, walking in the park, snow skiing, flower arranging, dinner and drinks with friends, participating in the arts, and chocolate chip cookie dough. Create your list of something new or exciting.

3. **Laugh or Smile 25 times per day** It can be infectious to others, so always greet another with a grin.

4. **Choose your Playmates & Playgrounds** Who can I get to play with me today? Where is the perfect playground? Maybe it is someone or somewhere old, new or just you.

5. **Have "Fun Money"** Hide money in your wallet. My mother used to give me a $100 bill and say, "Keep this with you in your billfold for something special and spontaneous."

6. **Schedule a "Pajama Day"** Take a day off, for real. Stay home in your PJs for 24 hours You deserve a break from being "on-the-go." Read fiction, watch movies or your favorite TV show, play games, take a hot bath, do nothing. I do this at least once a month to nourish my body and soul.

7. **Be Spontaneous and Open to new People, Places and Things** Try a new restaurant. Take a class, just for fun. Make a new friend. Travel somewhere new every year. My best friend enjoys playing bocce ball and singing karaoke. Start planning now.

8. **Engage in Nurturing Activities** What feeds your body and spirit? Spend time in nature, alone and with those you love. Personally, I enjoy massages and hiking.

9. **Start Planning the Big Stuff Now** Don't wait until the somedays… choose one item on your bucket list and start the planning now. Perhaps it's a big trip, so start a special account, block the time on your calendar, look at travel sites, join an organization that supports your dream. For example, I am a member of the Italian Cultural Institute of Louisville because I love Italy and want to keep learning about the culture between going on trips there.

There is no time to waste and you are in charge of creating your own playtime. Fun is a conscious choice. It is about giving yourself permission with both your thoughts and your actions to be happy and to enjoy life in the process of it unfolding. Frolicking and fun are different for everyone, so determine what you want. Decide to be happy every day, and then do the juicy, simple or perhaps bold things that will bring you exuberance, passion and pleasure.

## Coaching Questions to Inspire More Frolic, Fun and Play:

1.  Who are your playmates and where are your playgrounds?

2.  What life areas need more succulence and joy?

3.  Create a list of the things you want to do, big or small, with your free time and refer to it often.

# What's Possible?

*"What you believe and conceive you can achieve."*
Napoleon Hill

Where do you live? What occupies your mind and what do you think about most of the time? Are your thoughts positive and filled with hopes, wishes and dreams—or do you live with fear, doubt, anxiety and pessimism? Do you consider what's possible for you, your family, and your future? Or is it just "wishful thinking," with no real conviction or the assurance of a positive result?

There is a belief in the metaphysical world that there are unlimited possibilities in the physical world. There is enough for everyone, and that in order to attain success, you must start with that premise. I know that as a coach, I have held this perspective since I started my business in 2003... that there are enough clients for every coach who shows up, does great work and wants it. It is one of the reasons why I do not see other coaches as competition, but rather as colleagues, all doing important work to make a positive impact in the world. After all, I could not coach everyone, and quite frankly, am not the right coach for everyone. I am, however, a fantastic coach for someone who truly desires forward movement, wants to be inspired and create sustainable change in his or her life. I believe there are unlimited possibilities in what I can co-create with my clients and Excavive products. I have to believe in myself, my value in the world and the desired outcomes I want for my life to turn possibility into reality.

Imagine that the Universe is one giant mirror and it says yes to everything— every time you stay positive, you activate the energy around you to support what you are creating. And every time you doubt, you backslide into the reality of staying exactly where you are, or worse, fall further behind. The power of this positive and negative energy is alive and real. Think about when you begin your day in a good mood, and then as the day continues, you are with people who are having a tough day; ranting about the state of the economy or political landscape; or sharing their own personal challenges that never seem to get better. Do you notice how your mood changes, your joy diminishes, and you are left wondering what happened to your light? Consider the sources— people feed on negativity and the media favors the doom and gloom. Our minds are filled with the "what if's" of life, and we are programmed to expect the worst. No wonder it is difficult to keep your momentum and uphold your ideals. I ask you, is this type of thinking really helpful?

I am not suggesting that you put your head in the sand or do not have compassion and empathy for others, but rather I am asking you to recognize the energies that impact you. Stop giving away your vitality to others and choose who and what gets in. Be accountable for what you want to create, believe in and endorse. Protect your own energy and reject the naysayers of the world.

Look into your heart and ask yourself what is possible for your own life. Close your eyes, get quiet and still... what do you see or hear for yourself? What is your life purpose, and how do you want to fulfill that potential? Get clear on what you truly desire. Determine what is attainable and begin to take action that supports your intentions. Do something, anything towards what is possible. If you claim your dream and it does not happen, power on and keep the faith. Living in possibility means persevering, staying on task, not giving up on your goals, and continuing to show up until something different presents itself. Consider the statement, "this or something better." I will hold this possibility until I either accomplish it or am inspired to reach for a better vision. Consider the wisdom from American industrialist Henry Ford, "Whether you believe you can or whether you believe you can't, you are probably right." And the wise First Lady Eleanor Roosevelt said, "The future belongs to those who believe in the beauty of their dreams." Isn't it time you pay attention to your dreams, conceive your next biggest goal and go after it? Imagine all you want for your life… all that is within reach and within the bounds of possibility.

**Suggestions for Activating Unlimited Possibility:**

- Daydream, imagine and fantasize often.
- Heal and truly let go of the past.
- Be willing to be open, change, grow and evolve.
- Refute smallness, think big.
- Make positivity part of who you are.
- Eliminate any negative energy and influences, including the media, "energy vampires" and any bad thoughts.
- Eradicate fear, limiting beliefs and old stories.
- Gather evidence of the good that exists in your life.
- Replace doubt with certainty.
- Believe 100%, down to your bones, in every cell of your body.
- Get outside of yourself and have compassion for others.
- Don't be limited by your own thinking.
- Risk failing.
- Value yourself and what you are creating in the world.
- Take action steps that are aligned with your goals.
- Don't do the "should's."
- Create experiences that support your wishes.
- Be scared, take a deep breath and do it anyway.
- Be grateful, gracious and worthy.

German poet Johann Wolfgang von Goethe wrote, "What you can do, or dream you can do, begin it; boldness has genius, power and magic in it." I hope that you will exert the magic of possibilities in your life and realize the inevitable power in creating your reality. Here is a coaching exercise to guide you through this process.

## A Coaching Exercise to Make Your Dreams a Reality:

In order to manifest your dreams, it is important to get clear about what you really want. I suggest continuously recording your thoughts, as well as to reviewing your ideas on a consistent basis.

1. Spend 15 minutes every day thinking about your highest hopes.

2. Commit to your highest well-being and on a daily basis.

3. Replace limiting logic and beliefs with empowering knowing and ideas. Think about the positive outcomes. What do you want based on your deepest desired outcomes?

4. Eliminate anything that does not support your destiny, especially energy drains. Refute *all* negativity.

5. Think about the happiest times in your life. Successes? Courageous choices? What feelings were present? Write these down and access those emotions often.

6. Now, link your desires with your feelings. Create "It is possible that…" statements. Read your affirmations, take action and believe it to be so.

# Excavate Your Creative Self

*"The aim of art is to represent not the outward appearance of things, but their inward significance."*
Aristotle

When I attended my first life coaching training over in 2003, one of the first things I learned is that everyone is creative, resourceful and whole; and they have their answers inside themselves. I understood people were fully capable of finding solutions but what I did not recognize at the time is how powerful and provocative tapping into one's creative source can be.

For many people, their creativity takes a novice approach of doing artistic things when there is extra time, money and resources. Participating in an occasional art class, taking up a new hobby, redoing your home, taking photographs or dabbling in some out-of-the-ordinary projects at work are secondary to life's bigger demands of work, family and other obligations. So, creative pursuits are not necessarily prioritized, do not hold much importance or are non-existent.

At the other end of the spectrum are those who hold a dream, or are engaging in, the professional option of being an artist, designer, innovator, director, writer or trendsetter. Many of these creative types have a natural inclination or talent; are educated or trained in one or many specialties; are paid for their products and services; and continually engage in their artistry.

A third and final perspective on creativity lies somewhere in the middle where creativeness is part of everyday life and work, whether it is inventing new approaches to the current way of doing things or prioritizing at least one artistic endeavor because of the enjoyment it brings. For example, I took up flower arranging a few years ago— not because I want to open a florist but rather to engage in a creative activity that brings beauty to my world and others. When I am putting together a combination of different textures and colors, I feel a flow, a grounding, a swelling of energy, and pure bliss.

No matter where people fall on the originality scale, I believe everyone can reap enormous benefit from finding their own creative identity which is fundamental to being able to tap into passion, joy, and deep satisfaction. It only takes courageous confidence to move forward. So, where do you start? What does it take to awaken the dormant, creative soul?

Begin by getting self-empowered to use your imagination and dream about what you want to do next. Discover what you like and dislike; establish an expansive way of thinking outside of the box; utilize consistent habits that support your vision; nurture your inner inventor; commit to staying on the chosen path even when it gets hard; have creative collaborators for renewal and accountability; build a tool kit of supplies and resources so you are always prepared to capture your inspirations; and take forward-moving action each day. By engaging in these steps, you will set in motion a more colorful and vivid life. Below are some questions to get you inspired to claim what you want to create.

## 15 Questions to Excavate Your Creativity:

As you consider your own creative talents, it is important to give thought about how you tap into your own resourcefulness. The following questions are designed to stimulate your thinking about what ignites your passion and how your interactions in the world affect what you create.

1. What do you create and why?

2. From where do you get your inspiration and ideas?

3. How does your life reflect your creativity... in your home? Clothes? Hobbies? Relationships? Business?

4. What **unique** skills do you have that directly support your creativity? Name at least three.

5. What experiences make you feel most alive? List your passions.

6. How does color affect you? What colors do you like/dislike?

7. Think about when you are being your most creative...now describe your surroundings.

8. Do you have any "rituals" that prepare you for your project?

9. When is the best time of day for you to create?

10. Who supports your creativity? Do you have creative collaborators?

11. What distractions exist in your life that keeps you from being your most inspired self? List the things you do instead of creating.

12. How do you motivate yourself to start (or finish) a project?

13. Is there a common theme or element in your writing, designs, products or art?

14. What does your creativity say about you and how is it revealed in what you create?

15. What is the message you want to give your family, friends, community and the world through your creations?

Using your answers to the above questions, consider what creative projects you want to undertake. Identify two or three, choose the most provocative one, and initiate your new creative journey.

When you begin to recognize the things in your life that inspire you, you will begin to move more rapidly toward those things and create a synergy that allows your creativity to remain ever-present, alluringly alive and permissively playful. There is an artist inside of you and you only need to excavate the truest form of your own creativity. Albert Einstein said, "Imagination is more important than knowledge." I invite you to go on an inventive quest to learn about your creative self, and then pursue the ingenious things that make you happy.

# Own Your Feminine Power

*"The most common way people give up their power is by thinking they don't have any."*
Alice Walker

There is much talk about the feminine and what it means to be a feminist, and I can't help but wonder what that really means in today's world. As much advancement as women have made over the past few decades, it seems to me that we still struggle on what it means to be both powerful and tender at the same time.

We've made much progress since the ERA was ratified in 1977 and the uprising of the MeToo movement in 2017, yet there are still challenges for women in today's society both externally and internally. On the outside, we need to have more respect, a bigger seat at the table, honored for the work we do with equal pay and recognition for our contributions. Yet, within ourselves, we still need to find the right formula.

Many women still struggle with how to be seen, heard and taken seriously. There seems to be an on-going debate on how the feminine and masculine traits are supposed to show up for each gender. Traditionally, women have been the softer, more sensitive gender, and are often thought of as being nurturing yet weak in comparison to men. Men are known for their qualities of bravery, toughness and strength, as well as the role of "provider." No wonder people are confused!

How do you tap into your softer, feminine side and still remain effective in the masculine world of achieving, doing and accomplishing? And, what is it to be a strong feminine woman without been seen as a bitch? And for men, how do you show your empathic and caring side without been seen as lecherous?

There are many ways to connect to your truest self by encompassing and balancing both our masculine and feminine traits. I believe you can connect to your femininity by first honoring your senses on a continual basis. The five senses of seeing, hearing, touching, tasting and smelling will help you to tap into your feelings, your thoughts and your emotions. Delighting in your senses will create the awareness of what is right for you and being present in a strong body will allow you to be more open, sensitive and resilient. At the same time, it's important to build emotional, physical and mental fortitude.

You can also awaken your sixth sense, also known as intuition. This powerful intuition is an inner knowing, a small voice inside that allows you to know the truth before you reveal it to the outside world. It is your gut feeling, a place of peace, a sense of harmony and an all-knowing self-trust. Women are often credited with having better instincts, a very feminine trait. Yet, I think everyone can cultivate it. So, use your intuition— it is the pinnacle of your feminine power and wisdom.

And finally, I think everyone can benefit from compassionate power, nuanced complexities and wholly showing up with all of one's amazing qualities. Own your feminine power by being unapologetically willing to use your best traits and talents to better serve your world. And, don't make men wrong or break them down in order to be powerful… you can stand on your own, you just need to source your power from within. Here are some ways:

### 11 Ways to Source Your Feminine Power:

1. **Evolve Self-Trust** Develop your intuition. Follow your instincts and trust yourself. Meditate, journal and get quiet.

"Listen" to what is revealed and make courageous choices accordingly. Only you know what is true and right for you.

2. **Use the Five Senses** Savor the senses— touch, taste, smell, sight, hearing— to heighten your awareness and better tap into what is going on around you. Plus, it can improve your moods, and lead to a stronger intuition.

3. **Speak Up** Say how you feel, ask for what you need and want, and do so with kindness and compassion. Don't raise your voice to get your point across, but rather be strong, steady and direct. Let no mean no, and yes mean yes. And remember, there is power in silence.

4. **Live in Nuanced Perspectives** Expand your capacity to see many sides of a situation, the complexities and layers versus the black and white, linear thinking.

5. **Make White Spaces** Give yourself time to follow your energy, putter around, think, daydream, ponder, read, write… all without speaking or being spoken to. Flourish in the creative thoughts that arise. Schedule this on your calendar, if needed.

6. **Let Nature Be Your Guide** Go outside and observe, look for the wild feminine energy in nature. Breathe and smell the fresh air. Always choose scenic routes.

7. **Find Your Female Tribe** Find the women in your life who will be your biggest cheerleaders and fans. This is a place for vulnerability and sanctity, unconditional love and support. Mine shows up in several places personally and professionally, but first and foremost is my Blazing Blair Women group— my mother, my sister, my daughter, my

niece and my son's girlfriend. We have an on-going text chat and regular Zoom calls.

8. **Tune in to Your Body** Move your body, dance to the music. Workout and actually feel your muscles supporting you. Get regular touch through massage or other healthy practices.

9. **Design Your Sensual Surroundings** Choose a place of your own that is just for you, where you feel safe, womanly and exquisite. Find your "creative portals" or the place that you feel the most inspired. Create a "She Shed."

10. **Wear Beautiful Feminine Clothes** You want your clothes to make you feel like your best self. Use your favorite colors that truly reflect you and create the impact you want to make. Don't use only neutrals. Embrace any textile that makes you feel good. Wear dresses and skirts. Adorn yourself with your favorite jewelry and scarves. Use make-up. And, don't wear so much black.

11. **Embrace Compassionate Power** Lead with an open heart. Listen to others by being curious as opposed to having bullish energy. Learn to be strong without being a bitch. Be decisive, be in choice and never be a victim to your circumstances. Show your resiliency and gumption.

Supreme Court Justice Ruth Bader Ginsberg said it best, "Feminism… I think the simplest explanation, and one that captures the idea, is a song that Marlo Thomas sang, 'Free to Be You and Me.'" Give yourself, and others, permission to be authentic, powerful and free. And, listen to what is revealed about the poetry of your life through your intuition, for it is your true feminine power.

## Coaching Questions to Embrace Your Feminine Power:

1. Are you living in a way that truly expresses you and your soul? Be sure you are living *your* life.

2. What would it look like to land softer in your life? In other words, what if it were easy, light and playful?

3. In what ways do you need to re-balance the strong feminine within you? Do you need more or less of her?

# Be Tempted & Do Something About It

*"Unfulfilled desires are dangerous forces."*
Sarah Tarleton Colvin

What tempts you? Maybe it is the latest get-rich-quick scheme you read about on-line. Maybe it's sex, power or prestige. Or possibly it's money, possessions or a favorite dessert. When most people hear the word "temptation," it stirs up thoughts of a wild torrid affair, a piece of chocolate, playing hooky, or taking a spontaneous trip where you leave it all behind.

In our Judeo-Christian culture we often hear the Bible verse, "Lead us not into temptation, but deliver us from evil." So, I ask, does temptation always lead us to evil and are the things you want bad? Temptation has a bad reputation, and maybe for good reason, as sometimes there can be devastating consequences to the choices and actions made because of it. But I believe the things people want are not bad, it's the context or circumstances in which they want them. And it can inform them about a deeper unmet need or desire.

So, what do you long for? What if you could be curious about the fire that has been ignited within you? What if you could embrace the yearning long enough to see if the current opportunities could lead you into new growth? Maybe longing for passion is pointing you toward more intimacy with your partner or a hobby that feeds your soul. Wanting a new job could be about the desire for more freedom, autonomy and value. Perhaps your temptation is simply about the need to connect to yourself.

Part of my coaching technique allows me to help my clients examine their beliefs so they can make decisions about what to do with the things they crave most. Beliefs are created based on experiences and relationships, as well as how people have been shaped by family, teachers, religious or spiritual leaders, media and books. There are "rules" to play by, but sometimes even those need to be examined so that you can mature and discover your true authenticity. Beliefs are not good or bad; they either limit you and hold you back or empower you and move you forward.

So, be tempted, be curious about it and let it lead you to more fulfillment and joy. Here are some ways to deal with temptation and do something about it to move your life forward.

### Guidelines on Following Your Desires:

- **Wake Up** to what is being awakened within you. What passions need to be expressed? What or who is stirring your soul so much so that you feel like you are doing exactly what you are supposed to be doing?

- **Follow Your Urges** Take chances, activate courage and try something new just for the sake of it. Say "yes" as often as possible.

- **Be Conscious** about your decisions. You are always in choice with your attitude and thinking. Don't let fear be in charge.

- **Know Your Line** Be fierce for you and what you stand for. Stay true to yourself, and don't compromise. Say yes when you mean yes and no when you mean no. Also, know that you can move your line... just know how far and why you are moving it.

- **Listen to Your Body** Get quiet and let your body inform you. When we experience a sense of peace and comfort in our bodies, we are in alignment with our thoughts, feelings and decisions.

- **Cause No Harm** to yourself or others. There is no room for creating a life of guilt or future amends for yourself.

- **Savor Your Current Life** Find joy and appreciate all that you have and do. You might discover something new that already exists.

My clients tell me about their temptations and are often looking for someone to give them permission to follow their passions and dreams, to do something different. After making sure they are truly honoring themselves and are not causing harm to others, I say go for it while taking 100 percent responsibility for their choices and actions. I am not here to judge but rather hold them up. I give my clients their dignity by allowing them to make their choices, good and bad, and I hope they honor their conscience, sacred contracts, and commitments made with self, God and others. I am simply a catalyst for awareness, authenticity and action.

## Coaching Questions to Tempt Authenticity:

1. What is enticing and tantalizing enough to take big risks for your own happiness?

2. What is the distinction between feeling good and being fulfilled?

3. What are the "beliefs" or "rules" you have that are no longer serving you?

4. List five things that tempt you and give in to your healthy desires.

# Connect to Your Sexual Self

*"The fiery moments of a passionate experience
are moments of wholeness and totality."*
Anais Nin

Do you feel satisfied and connected to your sexual self? Are you
bonding with your partner in a deeply intimate physical way? Do
you have a passion-filled life that includes connection, creativity,
self-nurturance and love? Are you getting your sexual needs met
on a regular basis, whether you are with or without a partner? Sex
is important, *and* let me say upfront, it is not my job to judge,
regulate or put rules around morality—that is up to you and your
belief system. However, as a Life Coach, I assist others in discovering
how to achieve the most fulfilling life possible while maintaining
equilibrium. When thinking about life balance, the physical, sexual
and sensual needs are part of that formula as well.

As humans, physical intimacy is not only needed but also critical
for survival. The need to be touched, caressed and desired is real,
and it is essential to be aware of the sexual part of yourself that is
good, natural and powerful. Your sensuality is given the chance to
come alive when you are in your body while allowing your emotions
to be present. By understanding this part of yourself, you can tap
into your own passions and desires as well as channel your sexual
energy—whether it's having sex to deepen the connection with your
partner; to procreate and have children; or to give birth to a new way
of living or a creative project.

Being in charge of your sexual self gives you freedom and

independence, especially when you realize you are in control of your decisions and what is right for you. Most pleasure for women takes place above the waist, as we are highly emotional creatures, so it is important to be intellectually turned on. Physical cravings are often dictated by factors such as body image, mental and emotional stability, safety and trust in your partner, balanced hormones, a stress-free life and fulfillment in other existing areas. Making healthy choices not only creates physical pleasure and passion, but is also a form of empowerment, self-expression, imagination, and, more importantly, can deepen the spiritual intimacy with your partner and yourself.

One of the biggest problems I have observed regarding sex revolves around a person's self-worth. Too many times, I see people who give their power away sexually by not expressing their true desires. They don't have the confidence to ask for what they really want and need; compromise themselves to keep a relationship that is not right for them rather than be alone; have completely shut down their sexual selves; or use sex to feel validated, powerful or self-important. Perhaps past messages about sex such as "sex is bad," "good girls don't enjoy sex" or "having sex before marriage or outside a committed relationship is sleazy" add to the lack of worth.

However, recreating a strong self-esteem will give you sexual freedom and allow your passion to easily flow. And, being connected to your sexual self will enhance your self-love, self-worth, creativity, passion, connection and beauty. Here are some ways to build or re-build a robust sexual self-esteem.

## <u>Tips to Building a Robust Sexual Self-Esteem:</u>

- Understand what you really want and desire both sexually and in other areas of life.
- Discover as many of your passions as possible.
- Deepen your understanding of your sensual self by tapping into your five senses of smell, taste, sight, hearing and feeling.

- Choose a healthy lifestyle in order to be your physical best.
- Make eye contact, smile and exude confidence.
- Build a safe and trusting relationship where sex can flourish.
- Recognize the vulnerability, connecting and bonding aspects of sex.
- Be curious about what you do not know or are interested in.
- Become confident saying no and creating boundaries.
- Express yourself powerfully and lovingly.
- Foster self-confidence by feeling as good about your inner self as you do your outer self.
- Get to know your own body, your likes and dislikes.
- Follow your urges and be playfully spontaneous. Make love… A LOT.
- Strengthen your spiritual connection.
- Value a richly purposeful life, with or without a partner.

You have the right to a fantastic sex life. If you are currently satisfied, keep the flames burning. If not, and you desire sexual happiness, regain your sexual confidence by putting the focus on yourself first. Sex can be an area that can either build you up or break you down… get to know your sensual self and the empowerment that exists within you.

## A Provocative Exercise about Your Sensual & Sexual Self:

1. By answering the following questions, you can learn more about your sensual self and sexual needs:

    - Are you satisfied with your sex life? Your partner? What is the distinction between feeling good and being fulfilled both sexually and generally?

- Are you using sex to feel better about yourself and build a false sense of security; or to be expressive and create a connection?

- What are your beliefs about sex? What messages were you given while growing up that may no longer serve you?

- Are your actions authentically you? Are they life affirming or life numbing?

- Create your own definition of sexual integrity.

- Do you withhold yourself or settle for less in your sexual life and life in general? In what ways?

- Who are your favorite bewitching men/women, and what qualities do they possess that you could emanate?

2. Now, "right-size" sex in your life. In other words, assess where you are now, decide what you need, determine what's normal for you and give yourself permission to ask for what you want from yourself and your partner.

3. Choose three strategies that will strengthen your sexual self-esteem and start implementing those today.

# Unleash Your Inner Gypsy

*"The purpose of life is to live it, to taste it, to experience to the utmost, to reach out eagerly and without fear for newer and richer experience."*
Eleanor Roosevelt

For anyone who has read my previous book or magazine columns, you know I write about authenticity, what it means to be true to yourself, and how to truly live that in the world. I strive to empower and inspire the real you with my words of encouragement, my bold positions on various subjects, my helpful lists and my coaching exercises to get you involved in your process.

I imagine that many of you have taken some of my suggestions and are living better, happier and more joyful lives. But I wonder about those of you who would say to me, "I get it Jennifer, but how do I really get there?" "Being authentic makes sense, but where do I start?" Valid questions.... so instead of making my usual friendly suggestions, I am going to show you how I evolved more into myself through my own personal process.

Several years ago, when I was questioning the next place where I wanted to be personally and professionally. I had worked hard to grow my business and was happy with my life, yet I was yearning for more expansion, more adventure and more romance in my life. I wanted to melt away my own limitations I put on myself and allow more freedom to fully embrace my life.

Through being coached, I was inspired by the idea of gypsies, and I used the semblance of their lives to deepen my own path and to re-ignite my passions. To me, gypsies have qualities that I desired more of in my life, such as their beautiful, extravagant and playful look; the free-spirited dancing and love of music; their ability to move around the world uninhibited; and their sense of community. So, I used the gypsy-filled symbolism to inspire my own definition of freedom and passion in the world.

Don't get me wrong; I realize gypsies have a bad reputation, especially in today's modern world. They are known as nomads who take advantage of the people, places and things, and do not have much regard for others. However, their dreamy qualities gave me the portal to further explore how I wanted more freedom, passion, excitement, adventure and beauty in my life, and I coupled that with my personal responsibility and commitments to change my world. Created in July 2010, below are my own guidelines to a gypsy-filled life. I hope that it will inspire you to consider yours.

### Jennifer's Gypsy-Living Personal Guidelines:

*MUST include Personal Freedom, Passion, Excitement, Adventure, Beauty, & Being Cared For*

- Honor my free-spiritedness while still being responsible to my other commitments. There is room for both.
- Stay grounded and clear— never apologize for who I am, justifying only tears me down. Live my values every day.
- Bring confident, diva energy to my daily tasks. Speak up often!
- Make decisions that make me proud and excited as opposed to staying stuck or keeping the past going.
- Dance and listen to music as much as possible.
- Let my desires inform me, inspire me and move me forward to create great things in the world. Plan juicy adventures.
- Make life magical and have fun first. Each month try out or engage in at least one new thing.

- Choose experiences over material goods.
- Become more cultured. Participate in the worldly pleasures of good food (new restaurants), fine wine (a new drink), and the arts, especially visual arts, theater, opera, ballet, movies, etc. as often as possible. Ignite the senses. For example, choose a wine tasting over a networking meeting.
- Get fed artistically with play dates, art dates and field trips to museums everywhere. I now take contemporary art trips with my museum and have traveled to Cleveland, Los Angeles and Mexico City the past year.
- Each year visit a new place I have never experienced. (I started this over 15 years ago and have succeeded every year.)
- Bring love along for the journey. I look for ways to connect and share the learning as well as to be cared for and receive support from others along the way. I let go of relationships that hold me back, drain my energy or I just don't feel good in them.
- Include my children, loved ones and friends in my life adventures.
- Travel light. Liberate my physical spaces by cleaning out clutter, bringing in beautiful items and adding colors that inspire whatever emotion I want to feel that reflects my "inner gypsy."
- Wear bright, classy, feminine clothes and jewelry that reflect passion, beauty and movement. Do I feel beautifully connected to myself? Is this a reflection of my truest me?
- Maintain a home base. I need a soft place to land, a place to come home to and for me, it's my Louisville home, especially my pretty, serene bedroom.
- Everything must be beautiful, so make it pretty. No exceptions.
- Allow my adventures to inspire my creativity and to empower other people I serve in the world.
- Don't betray self or cause harm to others along the way.

- Create strong structures to support my adventure, freedom, growth and learning. (Financially, emotionally, physically, spiritually, professionally and relationally.)
- Rest when needed and never sacrifice self-care. Be intentional about rejuvenation.
- Generate fulfillment from within; don't depend on others for my own happiness.

You might be wondering if I actually embrace any of this, and the answer is yes— I do my best to live this and have had some amazing results. This energized me to publish my first book, to travel more internationally and get more involved in the arts in my hometown. I still long for more exotic adventures, more time with the people I love, consistent self-care and visiting more museums. Yet, I have created a life that honors and expands my rich values of freedom, personal power and beauty. As the writer William Shakespeare wrote, "To thine own self be true." I believe he was encouraging us to uncover our authentic selves and then live life to the fullest based on that true version.

## An Exercise in Excavating Your Own Gypsy Standards for Authenticity:

Using my list as a sample, create your own personal standards for living authentically. What do you long for? What does full, rich life look like? What will free you up? What is on your bucket list?

After completing your gypsy list, begin to integrate the items, one at a time until you have succeeded in bringing more personal freedom, adventure and fulfillment into your life. Create a list of affirmations or "I" statements to keep you grounded to who you are and how you show up in the world.

# ENHANCE YOUR WORK

Do you love what you do? Do you wake up excited about your day ahead? Are you filled with joy and enthusiasm, or dread and despair? If you are like many people, you are in a joyless job.

As a Coach, I am often hired to help someone find a new path to earning a living, supporting their families or pursuing a dream career. Sometimes, it's assisting with building more confidence to go for a promotion, re-entering the workforce after many years or becoming a better, more compassionate leader. Some feel stuck in their current situation, lack clarity on what's next or can solidify a valid plan to move forward, so I help them get there.

When it comes to examining your work, I think it's important to first define what "work" means. Some people define work as a productive activity or one's place of employment. Others describe their work as how they spend their days Monday through Friday. It can be paid or unpaid, with or without benefits, employed or self-employed. For instance, I consider stay-at-home parents as having an equally important job as the person going to an office. The important thing is to be able to define what it is you do that truly aligns with who you are, know your value, do it with excitement and joy while balancing the rest of your life. This can take time to discover how best to proceed, especially when one is dependent on their livelihood. I get it. It took me years to figure out my purpose doing something I love.

In my twenties, I worked in the corporate world and loved the creativity, the camaraderie and work itself. I was in corporate communications for many years. After a short stint as an education director for lawyers, I decided to become a stay-at-home mom when my children were young. During that decade, I realized I needed to feel more purposeful and I gave my time and talent to community causes while continuing to grow my skills and manage a household. After I divorced, I knew I would need to financially support myself, but was really torn about not being there for my children. So, in my early forties, I set out to discover my right livelihood that would give me the freedom to still be "Mom" coupled with doing something that I deeply cared about. My life experiences, the healing work I did and the fantastic teachers and training I had set me up to pursue an amazing career that I still love after almost twenty years.

Enhancing your work will allow you to discover the path that will make you the happiest while remaining true to yourself. Whether it's changing careers, retiring, re-entering the workforce, learning something new, becoming better in your current role, it's important to be happy. After all, you spend the majority of your waking hours at work while investing years of your life doing what you do... I think it's important to *really* love what you do.

In this section, I hope you will learn to be real at work, to love what you do, to set soulful goals, to better utilize your lists, to master your time, to cultivate prosperity, to embrace your strong side, to communicate powerfully, to lead compassionately and to claim your success. It's time for you to enhance your work by fully showing up, loving what you do and using your gifts and talents to positively impact the lives of others— no matter how you define work for you.

# Be Real at Work

*"Authenticity means erasing the gap between
what you firmly believe inside and what
you reveal to the world outside."*
Adam Grant

What is it to be your true self at work— not just the person filling a role, playing a part, acting professional or achieving a big project? Are you able to truly be your best and authentic self while maintaining professional credibility and influence?

For some people, they believe they must project a certain persona, subscribe to someone else's expectations, work extremely hard and "fake it until they make it" in order to get ahead. There is often no room for failure or there is a belief around sacrificing other parts of life in order to get ahead in their career. I get that determination and commitment are important, but not at the expense of who you truly are.

I believe there is a better way to be satisfied and achieve your professional goals; and it requires you to bring your real self to work each and every day. It is essential to be who you really are by engaging in your right livelihood using your true gifts and talents and making sure what you are doing aligns with your values. For instance, if you have a value of freedom but work in an environment that is not flexible, then you will be frustrated. Or, if you have a value of creativity but do not have a boss that celebrates and fosters creative thinking, and you do not speak up with new and innovative thoughts and ideas, you are not being your best and authentic self.

It is important be your authentic self whether you are at work, at home, with your friends or volunteering, but even more so in the workplace where you spend the majority of your waking hours each week. It also fosters compassion, connection and humanness in an environment where these things can often get left behind. So, you be you everywhere and in every situation. In the long run, it will serve you and the people you work with. Afterall, they will benefit from knowing and experiencing the real you. Here are several ways to remain your authentic self at work.

### Eight Ways to Keep it Real at the Office:

1. **Know Thyself** Understand and claim who you are, live in your strengths and values, and know why you do what you do. Your work must be about more than just money, power or position. You will attract more of the things that satisfy you, including recognition and prosperity, by bringing your authentic self to your work each and every day. Also, make sure your personal values align with your company values.

2. **Love What You Do** Are you excited about what you are doing? Does your career feel passionate and purposeful, or are you just earning a paycheck? If not, take the time to discover your calling and connect to what you do. Believe in your product or service and the success that only you can provide. Find joy and pleasure each day at your work. Lighten up, have fun and let your enthusiasm be contagious. People want to interact with happy, positive people.

3. **Convey Your Personal Brand** Believe in the product or service and the success that only you can provide, whether you work for yourself or someone else. Create a brand that clearly communicates your offerings, your core values and personal style if you work for yourself. If you work for a

company, see if their values are an extension of yours. And above all, let others see the real you.

4. **Create Connections** Build relationships by getting to know and understand the people you work with. What is important to them? Learn to relate to them as human beings with all of their strengths and struggles. Get to know their viewpoint, even if you don't agree with them. Be vulnerable and be generous in sharing who you are. And above all, practice kindness and respect.

5. **Be of Service** What service are you providing? What problem are you solving? Add value, offer a creative solution or fulfill a need. Get curious and create a reciprocity loop. Be giving and sharing because when you start the loop with someone it fosters connection and moves things forward. It makes others motivated to balance the scale...meaning they want to give back to you too. Use what you are blessed with and the world gets to benefit. Successful people give away lots of information, share their experiences and are willing to pay it forward. And, it's just good karma.

6. **Maintain Life Balance** Make self-care part of your business plan so you can bring your best body, mind and spirit to your tasks. My favorite metaphor for this concept is the rule to put on your own oxygen mask on an airplane before assisting those around you. Engage in what brings you joy and create a life you want, not just a business you pursue.

7. **Set Boundaries for Yourself and Others** Learn to say no and do it often. Speak up by asking for what you want. Stay intentional with your words and actions. Here is a tool I use: I create an energetic container for myself in which I decide who and what can come in such as collaboration, creativity

and connection, and who and what needs to stay out such as negativity, gossip, or mediocrity.

8. **Build Your Army of Advocates** Leaders know when to get help. You are not meant to go it alone. Even Solo-preneurs and creative people such as artists and writers need to build a support team of collaborators, mentors, advocates, and connecters. Be the expert in areas you excel and seek support for your struggles. My assistant maintains my database, newsletters, bank accounts, coaching log and other special projects. I have designers, tech support, writers, a coach— and my best friend and mother are on my "Excavive Board of Directors."

9. **Keep Going and Growing** Stay curious, learn new skills, expand your knowledge base and beware of becoming stagnant. Never let yourself be bored. Have the courage to keep moving your career or business forward by envisioning what next for you and your work.

10. **Know Your Worth** Find your confident you. Show up with self-assurance. Know you are worthy and do not accept anything less for yourself. And, ask for what you are truly worth when it comes to compensation and how you are treated.

American author Brené Brown states, "If you think dealing with issues of worthiness and authenticity and vulnerability are not worthwhile because there are more pressing issues, like the bottom line or attendance or standardized test scores, you are sadly, sadly mistaken. It underpins everything." Be real at work, and you and the world will benefit.

**Authentic Coaching Questions:**

1. Are you "you" while doing what you do? If not, what would make it congruent?

2. What excites you about your work?

3. What contribution are you making to the world?

# Love What You Do

*"It is the soul's duty to be loyal to its own desires.
It must abandon itself to its master passion."*
Rebecca West

Do you love your job? No kidding- do you really, really, really enjoy what you do? Do you wake up each day ready to embrace the opportunity to shine? Or, are you filled with dread and lack of motivation? Do you feel satisfied with your rewards and your contributions, or do you just get by, hoping that things will be different tomorrow?

Working is part of life, and for most people, it provides a way for people to take care of themselves and their families. It is also where people spend the majority of their waking hours. So, it is interesting to me as a Life Coach that so many people are so unhappy with what they do yet stay so long in their chosen roles. I often ask, "If you do not love what you do, then why do you do what you do?"

The reasons vary: to provide for themselves and their families; to have a certain lifestyle; to use their education, skills and training; to feel useful and make a contribution; to help others; to use their creativity; to support other passions; to invest in their future. People also stay in jobs because they feel stuck in a job, do not have the confidence or courage to change, or simply do not know what they really want to do. Where do you fall?

A person's work can play a large role in fulfilling a life purpose with meaning, passion and joy. I think it is important to enjoy what you do and if you do not, then you need to get fierce to find happiness in your work. You matter and your work matters, and people everywhere are longing for meaningful work where they are compensated for their full value. Many people find most of their self-worth in their work, and when it is off-track, self-esteem suffers. Although I do not endorse your work solely defining you, by finding the right fit, you can create a stronger sense of self and greater understanding of how you fit into a bigger picture of your life and the world.

I believe you can find joy in what you do every day by understanding yourself first, deciding what you want to do, and boldly positioning yourself for your best fit. Whether you stay at home with children, work in an office, start your own business, volunteer or are retired, it is not only vital to get your own needs met, but also to share your talents, wisdom and gifts with others so that they can benefit from your brilliance. Imagine... what would it be like to fully show up at your work- strong, powerful and excited about what you are doing, really be happy with your accomplishments, synergize those around you to also be their best and then be rewarded for a job well done that you actually enjoy?

It is up to you to determine your best career path as well as choose how you want to show up each and every day... strong or weak, engaged or detached, helpful or hurtful, excited or depressed? Love what you do and get the most out of your profession, whether you are in transition or have your dream job. Regardless, of where you are on your career path, here are nine secrets to assist you in ultimately loving what you do each and every day.

## Nine Requirements for Loving What You Do:

1. **Align your work with your personal values and self-worth.** Connect to your own uniqueness and be authentically true to yourself. Get paid what you are worth and use your assets, strengths, skills and voice at work. For example, if you value learning, take responsibility for your own growth

and learning even if it is not being offered to you, take a class or workshop. If you have a value of beauty, make your surroundings inspiring to you.

2. **Bring your passionate best.** Know what makes you come alive and be excited. Be present and put your stake in the ground. Use your voice and communicate clearly and passionately. What is it that you can't not do?

3. **Make self-care part of your business plan.** Live a balanced life; set aside down time, use all of your vacation time and take advantage of your benefits. Be sure to put your workouts, meditation and anything else that helps you be the fabulous you on your calendar each week. Have down time as needed.

4. **Have a positive mindset.** Write daily affirmations and choose to be happy, positive and engaged. Bring your heart to work with you and show compassion to others. Be responsible for the personal impact you bring to work. Never be a victim to a job you think you are supposed to keep, and proactively create an exit strategy if it is not working.

5. **Make meaning in what you do.** Finding the right work can create a stronger sense of self and greater understanding of how you fit into a bigger picture of your life and the world. A person's job can play a large role in fulfilling a life purpose with meaning, passion and joy. It is not only vital to find authentic meaning in what you do but also then understand your circle of influence so that you can share your wisdom and gifts with others so that they can benefit from your brilliance.

6. **Find your people: mentors, advocates, collaborators and soulmates.** Engaging in what you love to do and fully expressing that with courage ignites enthusiasm. Building bridges with the others, being contagiously passionate and authentically engaged raises the bar for everyone else and positively impacts the people around you. Seek connection with others who have similar values and be sure to protect your energy by staying out of negativity, office drama and gossip. Learn what you do not know and ask for feedback or help.

7. **Ignite your creativity** in as many aspects of your job as possible. Learn something new that interests you and find new ways to solve old problems. Engage your creativity at work and at home in as many life areas as possible. It will make you happier. (For ideas, see my chapter "Excavate Your Creativity")

8. **Understand what makes you feel valued and successful.** Is it words of affirmation, a title or promotion, more money? Validate your own self-worth and ask for what you need from others. Create a feedback loop for validation if you need it- most people want to be appreciated and recognized for their hard work. Get paid what you are worth.

9. **Know where you are going.** What's your end game? Define your personal why and what it is leading you to. Create a vision, set goals and make a personal growth plan for your career

I hope you actually like what you do. In fact, I want you to adore what you do each and every day... because when you are at your best, it feels like play and everyone benefits. Confucius said,

"Choose a job you love, and you will never have to work a day in your life." Are you ready?

## A Coaching Exercise to Enrich Your Work Life:

Do you adore your work? If not, what's missing? An exercise I use with my Life Coaching clients when we work on their career is a Wheel of Career that examines the level of happiness and satisfaction in twelve major areas of their work; or if you are not in a job, the priorities you have for one. This process provides perspective, balance and focus on what is working and what might need attention.

In each of these areas, rate your level of satisfaction on a scale of 1-10:

- Positive Outlook & Attitude
- Goals & Future Vision
- Money & Benefits
- Relationships & Collaboration
- Creativity, Passion & Fun
- Intellect, Learning & Growth
- Communication & Resolving Conflict
- Meaningful Work & Serving Others
- Authority & Responsibility
- Recognition & Belonging
- Mentors
- Office Space

Now that you have examined your career situation, what are three steps you could take immediately to either find more satisfaction in your current role, or begin to discover what's next?

# Set Soulful Goals

*"When we are motivated by goals that have deep meaning, by dreams that need completion, by pure love that needs expressing, then we truly live life."*
Greg Anderson

It's time to begin again…the beginning of another year, a birthday (my new year) or simply a time to reflect and start over— claim your new resolutions, set soulful goals, clarify intentions, and renew the possibility to really achieve all that you want in your life… you know, the really, really big stuff. A new career, launching a new business, financial freedom, meaningful relationships, a healthier body, romance, creative pursuits, you get to choose.

I love the process of continually re-launching a life vision by checking in on what has been accomplished, asking the questions about where you are now, and then envisioning the future based on the continual growth and learning that happens as each year passes. I am inspired by imaginative actions that lead to marvelous joy, expansive vitality and stunning success.

Setting goals is important in giving meaning and creating a focal point for what is next, especially when you are clear, decisive and focused about what attaining them will mean for you and others. By understanding your purpose and being clear about what you will get more of, such as love, joy, passion or security, it will then be easier to move toward soulful achievements.

Yet, as I write this, I wonder— why is it that some people can stay on a clear path of manifestation and stay true to the efforts to attain their dreams with balance and ease, and others can't? What does it ultimately take to remain focused and keep going toward their aspirations when it sometimes seems unattainable, frustrating, too hard or flat out hopeless? What's the secret to the success that many people seem to have mastered, yet has completely evaded others? Is it luck and the stars finally aligning? Is it powering on with hard work and perseverance?

Those qualities can be part of the success formula: claiming the vision, doing the work to back up the goal and sometimes allowing fate to play a part. You might also need to let go of something else first in order to make room for the new ideas and dreams. But more importantly, I think the secret ingredient missing for many people who don't reach their goals is the lack of *believing* that they can really achieve what they want.

Magic happens when you can source what you want from your own heart and soul, completely believing it exists, and accepting nothing less for yourself than the best possible outcome. Believe that you will get that promotion or successfully launch that new business. Trust that the career you love will bring you abundance. Accept that your friends are tried and true. Envision a healthy, fit and fabulous body. Believe you can publish a best-selling book.

As a Life Coach, I am hired to assist my clients in achieving their goals in an authentic and sustainable way that honors their goals as well as their authenticity. Think about any area of your life that you would like to change. What would you like to accomplish? Do these goals excite and expand you? Do you whole-heartedly believe you can reach these?

Part of the process includes examining your belief systems to see if your thoughts are empowering and moving you forward or limiting and holding you back. As you consider what's next for you, I challenge you to look at eight main life areas, consider your goals in these and then before you take any action, determine if your beliefs will support your dreams. Here are eight life areas to believe in.

## Eight Soulful Areas to Consider when Creating Goals:

1. **Career & Education** Why do you do what you do? What makes you satisfied in your work? Do you believe in what you are doing? Are you enjoying it? Are achieving what you want? Discover what makes you satisfied in your work and make sure the rewards match the job. If not, explore new possibilities.

2. **Money** Do you believe in abundance and that money is plentiful, or is tight and scarce? Does money come easily or does money evade you, causing you to doubt your own worth? Money goals are important, but so are your thoughts around abundance.

3. **Health & Wellness** Does your body support your work? Do you make time to take care of it with adequate sleep, nutrition, exercise, medical check-ups and positive thinking?

4. **Friends & Family** Do you invest in your relationships so that you can feel supported in what you do in the world? Take time for your tribe and give as much as you receive. Let the people in your life sustain you and your dreams. And, let go of (or redesign) the friendships that no longer work for you.

5. **Romantic Relationship** Does your partner support your work? Melt away old relationships, resentments, patterns and bad habits in order to keep your heart open. And, if you are single and want a partner, do you believe he or she really exists or, can you be happy with or without someone in your life?

6. **Personal Growth, Spirituality & Religion** Let your faith and beliefs serve you on a daily basis. Give up the ones that

hinder you or no longer align with who you have become. Create rituals and daily practices that support your success.

7. **Fun & Play** Feed your soul by carving out time to play or learn something new. It is in this playtime that my best creative business ideas show up. Plan the big and small adventures. And don't wait for the "some days" as life is short. Choose your playmates and playgrounds.

8. **Physical Spaces** Does your space reflect you? Do you have a problem with clutter? What stuff needs to be thrown away, donated or sold in order to open up space for the things you want— new clients, a space to write your novel, a place to inspire your creative thinking, a place you can be efficient, organized and productive.

Confidently launch your dreams and go forward with determination, clarity and a new solid vision. Henry David Thoreau wrote, "Go confidently in the direction of your dreams. Live the life you have imagined." With new beginnings, look into your heart and create an exquisite vision that honors you and the enchanting life you want, one that includes a fulfilling career, financial freedom, awakened creativity, a healthy body, a satisfying relationship, and a full life. Whatever you choose, you must believe it.

**A Soulful Goal Setting Process:**

Think about any area of your life that you would like to change. What would you like to accomplish next month, year or five years? Do these goals excite and expand you? Once you reach your goals, what will they give you? The following questions will assist you in excavating your next best steps to achieving your aspirations.

1. What are the TOP three things you accomplished in _____? Name your biggest successes.

2. Name three things you wanted to accomplish but didn't.

3. What is your next biggest dream or vision? Is it compelling or inspiring?

4. If everything is possible, identify <u>ONE</u> thing you'd like to be able to say about your life in one year that you can't say today. What is your expected outcome?

5. Name your goals and be as specific as possible.

6. What resources do you have today that will assist you in reaching your goals?

7. What will keep you from reaching your goals? Name "your stoppers."

8. Create forward movement by taking each goal and naming three inspired action items for each.

9. Who will you be accountable to and ask for support?

10. How will you reward yourself and celebrate?

# Let the Power of Listing Serve You

*"Written goals have a way of transforming wishes
into wants; can'ts into cans; dreams into plans;
and plans into reality. Don't just think it-ink it!"*
Dan Zadra

How many lists do you make over and over again? Things to do.
Errands to run. Groceries to buy. Work tasks to be completed. Goals
to set. Calls to return. School supplies, clothes and gifts to purchase.
Home repairs to be scheduled. Vacations to plan…the daily, weekly,
monthly and yearly lists can be endless.

I have observed that people's lives are run by their "to do" lists.
They make long, detailed lists, often adding an unrealistic number
of items to be completed in a short timeframe. I see clients focus on
what is not done rather than celebrate what gets completed. When
they do finish a job, they are so focused on moving forward to the
next item that they give little thought or recognition for a job well
done. Their sense of accomplishment, even self-worth, is determined
by the number items they check off on a regular basis, instead of the
quality and balance they are bringing to their overall lives.

Are you being realistic about your lists and the role they play in
your life? How many lists do you create, what is on them, and how
much time do you allocate? Do you consider if an item really needs
to be on the list? Many people sacrifice what is most important to
them, such as "me" time to rejuvenate or an occasion to connect
with others, simply because they are driven to get one more thing
crossed off.

These out-of-control "bad lists" are not good for you and can create a lot of added stress. On the other hand, some lists can be truly helpful by providing order, a "place holder" or a mind clearing. I challenge you to think about how you can be in charge of your lists, your time and your life by organizing and simplifying what you do. Here are my suggestions for more effective list making, as well as how to use list to create my positivity on your life.

**<u>Three Favorite Listing Habits:</u>**

1. **<u>Brain Dump</u>** Use a blank notepad and write down everything that comes to mind, dump it all. Thoughts, tasks, feelings, goals, dreams, desires. Big or small, anything and everything... this is a mind-clearing. It allows you to capture your thoughts while also freeing up space for my substantive and creative ideas and solutions. Do this as often as you like but remember this is not necessarily a master to do list. I suggest taking this brain dump and either discarding it or using it to create realistic and re-organized tasks.

2. **<u>"Post-It Note"</u>** It Put each item on a Post-it note and stick it on the wall. This "displayed thinking" allows you to move items around to group together, to look at what needs to be done next or even see pieces of a bigger picture. It can give you a fresh perspective, new priorities and better organization of your thoughts and action items.

3. **<u>Pick Three</u>** Take a master list and choose only the top three things you want to accomplish each day. Ask yourself the question, "When I get to the end of the day, what do I want to feel good about?" It is not necessary to have 25 items on a daily list, and you can get more done by focusing on what is most important in helping you achieve your goals. If you finish your top three and still have energy, then do

another three— keeping your list small will help you to better manage your time and energy, and you will feel more accomplished at the end of the day. Share your "pick three" with your best friend or partner at the end of each day.

## Three Lists to Invoke Positivity:

1. **Gratitude List** Write down who and what you are grateful for every day. I write this in the form of blessings and keep it in a daily journal. Be sure to share it with others.

2. **Accomplishment List** Keep an on-going list of things you have done over the past year (or several years) so you can see how far you have come. Add to it often and embrace your fabulousness.

3. **Dream List** Envision your dreams by brainstorming a list, mind-mapping or creating a vision that embraces who you want to be and where you want to go. List your desires through journaling, making vision boards or putting your items in a dream box. Claim what you want.

Transforming your list into something useful and "right-sizing" it relative to the realities of your life will give you a fresh perspective and more energy to achieve what you want. Follow your rhythm by knowing when you are most productive and align your actions accordingly. Good lists serve as focused reminders, goal setting, next steps and processes, mind de-clutterers, creative outlets or assistance to embracing all that you have and still desire to achieve. Make sure you are in command of your lists and, ultimately, your life. Let the power of listing serve you, not enslave you.

## Coaching Questions to Consider When Creating Lists:

1. How will "this item" move you forward?

2. Is there "something" on the list that can be done tomorrow in order to create more space for you today?

3. Are there any should's that can be removed or delegated? Is there something on your list you need to "out-source?"

4. Will doing "this task" bring you joy?

# Master Your Time

*"Time stays long enough for anyone who will use it."*
Leonardo da Vinci

Are you a person who believes you never have enough time? Do you plan, organize, agonize and fret over the many things on your to do list, only to get to the end of the day and feel defeated because what you got accomplished was far less than what's still ahead? Do you find yourself saying, "someday," "when I get more time" or even "I just don't have time for *xyz*?" If so, you are not alone.

One of the biggest complaints I hear from my coaching clients is that they do not have enough time to get everything done. And, the truth is, they are right. I truly believe the master "to do list" never gets complete. There will always be another meeting to attend, a new marketing strategy to create, a new program to launch, a new way to do business. That is one of the cool things about your work, there will always be something new to learn, an enhanced skill to acquire, a new role to attain, more money to make or actualizing a new idea. So, how we choose to manage our time both professionally and personally becomes a matter of prioritizing and choosing, with some added tools to help us along the way.

Time will always be an issue for those people who do not learn to find their best rhythm, live in their own authentic values and strengths, set boundaries and be intentional with the time they do have. It is essential that they understand what's most needed, and be able to ask themselves, "What's the next best step, every step of the way?" You only need to do the next right thing toward what you are creating.

## 13 Tools to Manage Your Time Effectively:

How can you find more time? What would you do with "extra" time you free up?

1. **Start with the big picture in mind.** Do you know what you really want? And, what you will get one you get there? What's the compelling reason to make this choice with your time? Create a vision or goal and make sure what you are doing fits in with the big picture. Devote time to your dreams.

2. **Know your strengths and values.** Understand what you are really good at doing and what you want to do. What is your native genius and your unique skills that you can apply to what you are doing? Choose to do tasks that align with these.

3. **Prioritize.** Create a Life List and make sure you ask yourself, "Is this what I want?" Be sure you are working on the things that will move you forward towards your dreams, and not just the smaller tasks that are sometimes the filler. For instance, if you want to publish a book, then make sure you are writing consistently, and not just thinking about it.

4. **Use a Brain Dump** to get out of the spinning in your head. Write everything down by thinking it and inking it. By clearing your mind of everything that is in it, you will be able to better focus on what you really need to be doing.

5. **Create Structures.** Structure creates freedom and gives you a way to proceed.

- *Daily Planning Time*: Set aside 15 minutes at the beginning or end of each day to decide what you want to get done the following day and reflect on how you did with the time you had.
- *Pick 3* things to accomplish each day. If you complete that, then you can decide if you want to start three more action items.
- Set aside a *Daily Oasis* for self-reflection, creative thinking and brainstorming, at least 10-20 minutes. You might even do this while walking in nature, journaling, taking a bubble bath or during a morning or evening ritual.
- Schedule your *Non-Negotiables* first such as self-care, family time, exercise and spiritual practices. Then fill up the rest of your calendar with the things that will maximize the time you do have.

6. **Get started.** Don't become paralyzed by not knowing what to do or letting fear take over. Do something, anything—just get going and you can adjust your plans along the way.

7. **Make Expectations Real.**
   - Break down projects into smaller tasks.
   - Employ the cumulative effect by spending a minimal amount of time each day on a project. This works well if you have a really large project.
   - Ready, set, go. Use a timer for 15-20 minutes and then decide if you want to do another round.
   - Deal with something once.

8. **Learn to say no often.** Set boundaries and limit interruptions, including e-mail, texts and phone calls. You might have to create your own set of "rules" on how often you check your devices. And remember, when you say no

to something— you are saying yes to something else, and vice versa.

9. **Be Present**. Do one thing at a time, being fully present in that moment. No multi-tasking, please. You will ultimately be more efficient, more effective and even more creative.

10. **Ask for help** Enlist others or hire someone to help you. Seek the guidance and counsel of others, both in and out of your chosen work. Learn from others. Getting another person's insight into a situation, problem or next step might save you time in the long run.

11. **Delegate** Is there someone else who could do this better or more efficiently than you? Who is really the best person to get the job/task done? Delegating will free you up to work on the things you are best at and love doing. And learn to let go.

12. **Be proactive, not reactive** with the tasks you need to get done instead of reacting to the demands of others. Plan ahead when possible and remember… another person's lack of organization or poor planning should not constitute a crisis for you.

13. **Done is better than perfect.** This one is for those of you who live in the land of perfectionism. You might consider learning when you can apply this suggestion.

Give yourself the gift of learning to how to master your own time. Consider ways to streamline your work as well as how to find the most enjoyment by being present to what you are really doing. As author Emily Dickinson wrote, "Forever is composed of now's."

## Coaching Exercise to Master Your Time:

Do you know where you spend your time? Are you enjoying what you do and are you getting accomplished what you want?

**Assess:** Begin by taking a week or two (or even a month) and track where your time goes. I suggest that you color-coded categories on your calendar or an excel sheet with the various life activities, such as work, exercise, sleep, family time, social time, self-care, hobbies/community service, worship, errands… anything that is important to you. There are also APPs that can assist you with this exploration.

**Discover:** Make a list of all of the things that need to be done, including those items you want to do but don't get around to doing or experiencing. What balance is needed now?

**Activate:** Using the tools above, be proactive by removing things that no longer align and begin with scheduling things that are most important to you such as self-care or relationship time. You can then fill in the rest of your tasks with what else is needed. And finally, don't forget to leave some blank spaces to deal with the unexpected or to have a little extra dream time.

# Cultivate Prosperity

*"I gain strength, courage and confidence by every experience in which I must stop and look fear in the face... I say to myself; I've lived through this and can take the next thing that comes along. We must do the things we think we cannot do."*
Eleanor Roosevelt

So, what do you really think about money? Do you feel wealthy, live in abundance and believe there is plenty to go around? Or, are you always worrying about money, scared of it, or don't even really understand it?

Abundance can mean different things to different people and can include both the tangible and intangible areas of life. Concrete achievements like a successful career, a beautiful home, financial accumulation, a great wardrobe and a fit body, as well as the non-physical richness of passion, loving relationships, creative pursuits, a Spiritual connection and serving others are all important. Living abundantly encompasses creating and balancing your definition of wealth relationally, spiritually, mentally, emotionally, physically and financially. The most challenging of these areas for many people is around money and their thoughts about financial success.

As a coach, I often ask people about their level of satisfaction when it comes to money? Are they happy with the money part of their lives, do they spend time with their resources and what does money do for them? Many people believe there is an unlimited amount of money to be made, more is coming, and they know how to manifest it for themselves. Others feel savvy with their structures such as savings, investments and planning. They have a healthy relationship and respect for money, theirs and others, and they spend time nurturing that financial relationship.

But there are those who do not have the confidence around wealth. They live in fear, lack and scarcity, and always worry that there is never enough. Many people strive for financial security yet are unclear about what that really looks like. I love author and coach Laura Berman Fortgang's definition of financial security in her book *The Prosperity Plan*. In her research she interviewed millionaires and she writes that they all said that financial security is "knowing they can start over if they had to have to. Their security did not come from their financial cushions, but rather it came from believing in themselves." So, creating abundance starts with the belief that you will be okay, no matter what happens, and that you have inner strength, courage and conviction to do what is needed- what a powerful thought!

So, how do you get in an abundant mindset? All things start with a thought, including your path to prosperity. When I work with my clients, I ask what is important to them around goals, wealth and their thoughts about money— what it means to them, how they receive it and what it does for them. When clients hit a block, it is often in the form of a self-limiting belief or fear that must be turned around in order to keep them moving forward. Below are some of the common constraining beliefs around money that I encounter…. and how they can be transformed. Feel free to create your own thoughts, affirmations and inspired actions around money.

## Transforming Scarcity Beliefs into Empowering Action:

**"I can't make enough money to support myself doing what I love and am passionate about."** If you do what is of service and of value to yourself and others, and you are taking the right actions, the money will show up.

*New Thought: "I make plenty of money in my right livelihood, doing what I love every day. I take inspired action on a consistent basis to live my best life."*

**"The Bag Lady Syndrome"** Are you living with the daily fear of going broke and ending up living on the streets when TODAY you are okay? Take action as a creative, empowered, and resourceful individual, so that you are in charge of your fate.
*New Thought: "I am safe now and always, and live in abundance. Every day I take action for my well-being and know that today I am okay. My creativity is creating my wealth."*

**"I feel guilty for wanting nice things."** If your intent around a purchase is because you love something, it brings you joy and you can afford it, then why not? If it is to impress others, "keep up with the Jones's" or complete a facade, then think again.
*New thought: "I love quality, beauty and can easily afford the things I want and desire. I work hard for the things and experiences I want. Today I did ____ towards my dreams."*

**"I need to take care of everyone else first, and then I will get to me later."** Are you being a victim to your spouse, your children or your friends? If you do not take care of you, then who will? Putting you first by prioritizing your self-care and the costs associated with it are imperative. Get pampered, replenished and nourished because that will allow you to fill up your tanks and enable you to show up fully when you are needed.
*New Thought: "By taking care of me first, I have more to give to others. I started my day with self-care and had plenty of time, money and energy for everything. Self-care is part of my business plan."*

**"I will do that someday when I have more time and money."** What are you waiting for? Life is short and happening now; and you may not get the opportunity, time, money or energy later. Only today is a certainty.

*New Thought: "I am grateful for today and live in the present moment. Today, I started making concrete plans to experience _____."*

**"I can't charge that rate! People cannot afford me and will not hire me."** Know your personal value, what you stand for, what the market can bear and who you serve. Put the appropriate value on your products, services, time and talent. Don't expect other people to value you if you do not value yourself, so ask for what you are worth. *New Thought: "I deserve to be paid what I am worth, and money is flowing to me easily."*

**<u>A Coaching Exercise to Increase Your Abundant Thinking:</u>**

Scarcity thinking can be a hindrance and bad habit. When you visualize your success and begin to think abundantly, you can increase your ability to manifest your true aspirations. So, let's practice thinking about possibilities, dreams and desires.

If you were to find an extra **$10** today, what would you do with that money? Would you treat yourself to a latte?

Now let's multiply that by 10 ... how would you spend **$100**? A special gift or experience for you, your partner or your family?

Again, let's 10 times that number to **$1,000**... what would you buy, save or give away?

Once more, let's multiply it by 10 and consider what you would do with **$10,000**? A dream vacation, a new career, increased savings, or pay off some debt?

Starting with **$100,000**, what's next? Would you pay down your mortgage, put away money for college, retirement, or a business investment?

Finally, **$1,000,000** to create your dreams… how would you fully step into living abundantly?

Now, choose your dream and start seeing, feeling, imprinting and believing in your own wealth. Take action and collect the evidence of your abundance along the way. When fear, self-doubt or old stories arise, learn to replace the disempowering thoughts with new, positive thought patterns and you will begin to appreciate your own greatness. Remember, your thoughts, good or bad, create your reality because the subconscious mind will always do the messages that are being sent to it. So, cultivate prosperity by creating a healthy and wealthy mind… there is no limit to what you can do.

# Embrace Your Inner Dude

*"To give anything less than your best is to sacrifice the gift."*
Steve Prefontaine

Women, generally speaking, are kind, compassionate, patient, nurturing, generous, sweet (most of the time) and tend to provide unconditional love. Yes, we are the soft souls that provide the heart-warming gentleness to our families, friends and partners. Yet, we can be doormats, suffer in silence, become martyrs to our circumstances, and tend to put our lives on hold—all for the sake of others. Don't get me wrong, I think women are amazing at juggling it all, and mostly being successful at it. Yet, we sometimes lack the drive, self-confidence and gumption men seem to pull off so easily.

One of the recurring themes I coach on is assisting women in rebuilding their confidence, self-worth, value and self-esteem. It seems to be a bigger issue with women than men. For example, last year I worked with a client on creating strategies for her to ask for a raise. She made the comment that other men in her office had asked for what they wanted easily, directly, expectantly, unemotionally, without hesitation and had a sense of detachment that translated into "of course I am worth it." They got what they wanted. So, I suggested that she take the same approach, and not only was it effective, but it was also easy.

This leads me to ask the questions, what can you learn from your male counterparts? How can you aggressively go for what you really want and vanish the victimization? Isn't it time to stop over-analyzing and get going? I think some of the answers can be found in lessons you can learn from guys, thereby, "embracing your inner dude."

## 10 "Macho" Traits to Take On:

1. **Persuasive Power** Men are natural born leaders, and do not question their individuality. They have the ability to use not only their external resources, but also access and activate their internal gifts and talents. Take the initiative, get empowered and use that power to create greatness.

2. **Physical Strength** Men stay committed to being active through working out and athletic endeavors to keep up their physical well-being, youthful energy and stress relief.

3. **Rational Reasoning** Men are less emotional when processing things and would never cry in the face of adversity. They are able to be objective, see the bottom-line and tend to be much more logical and practical.

4. **Bold Bravery** Men have the courage gene. Even if they are scared, it is not as obvious, especially when it comes to going for what they want both personally and professionally.

5. **Basic Simplicity** Men know who they are and what they do. Plain and simple. It's not complicated for them.

6. **Decisive Assertiveness** Men put their stake in the ground and continue moving towards that truth. Men seem to make a decision and move on, whereas women tend to dwell on decisions and question themselves after the fact. Stand up for what you think is right, and say it out loud with confidence, effectiveness and intensity... and don't look back.

7. **The Lighter Side** Lighten up... dudes don't worry as much. Keep it simple and consider giving up the agony of decision-making, guilt, shame and attachments.

8. **Action-Based Opportunities** Men generally want things to move along and go forward. They don't ask for permission; they take action, adjust, and keep going so as to not miss out. If needed, they will ask for forgiveness later.

9. **Sense of Adventure** Men follow their urges and are playful, spontaneous, independent, sexual and free-spirited. They say when, not if.

10. **The Visionary** Men tend to hold a big picture vision, are success-oriented, see where they are going and maintain what it will look like when they get there. Their vigilance and focus are unshakable, and it allows them to stay on task.

It is not my intent in this chapter to over-generalize or segregate the sexes, but rather to provoke thought and learning from each other. I am not suggesting that you stop being who you are or give up the goodness that already exists, as everyone needs both energies. There is no right or wrong with the sexes, just differences to embrace. The key is to integrate the best qualities of both men and women. And, the truth is, men have a strength and power that women often struggle with owning, and with a little work, they can harness and transform their own power into productivity and prominence.

**A Coaching Exercise to Excavate Your Maleness:**

1. Think about two or three men who you admire or who motivate you? What qualities do they possess of which you would like more?

2. When and to whom do you give your power away? Is there an opportunity to use some "male" traits to change this dynamic? Choose one bold characteristic and practice it as much as possible.

3. Now, balance your life by fully integrating your masculine and feminine traits in as many areas as possible. Assess where you are now, decide what you need and what your new "normal" needs to be. Ask for what you want from yourself and others, using ALL the traits needed to be your best you. Some examples... do you need to be:
   • More caring at the office?
   • More vocal at home?
   • More self-assured in your relationships?
   • Bolder in your creativity?

4. Choose three brave strategies that will strengthen your self-esteem and start implementing those today.

5. Finally, and most importantly, don't forget to thank the men in your life *often*. They need to feel appreciated for all that they do to support you and your greatness.

# Make Your Words Stick

*"Use every letter you write, every conversation you have, every meeting you attend, to express your fundamental beliefs and dreams. Affirm to others the vision of the world you want. You are a free, immensely powerful source of life and goodness. Affirm it. Spread it. Radiate it. Think day and night about it and you will see a miracle happen: the greatness of your own life."*
Robert Muller

Do you say what you mean and mean what you say? Do you feel like you are not only heard but also understood? Are your communication skills sharp and effective? In other words, do you get what you ask for? I often find that people, especially women, lack the skills to truly get their message across.

Sometimes it's a self-worth issue. Women often don't believe they deserve so they hold back, falling short in conveying what they truly mean or making a full request. Perhaps they are holding on to old messages such as women "should be seen, not heard." Other times, they simply lack solid tools to use their voice, and ultimately, their personal and professional relationships suffer. To create solid connections with others, it is important to learn how to communicate well. In doing so, you will get what you need, create stronger relationships, support efficiency, build trust, create a feedback loop, enhance your self-esteem, and feel energized and synergized.

The art of learning to convey information, thoughts, feelings, desires and opinions while at the same time creating the intended impact is a skill that can be developed and nurtured. Everyone is in relation to someone else, so having the ability to say what you want, when you want and be heard on the other side without being reactive, withholding, or fearing judgment benefits everyone.

Our words, spoken or written, are powerful, and can build up or tear down. The right words can create trust, loyalty, commitment, enthusiasm, love, healing and a deeper bond. Think about how you feel when someone genuinely says to you "thank you," "please," "I appreciate you," "great job," "I love you" or "I'm sorry." But when the wrong words are imparted, such as "you should have..." or "I am disappointed in you," it can be harmful, even devastating. So, choose your words wisely.

I once had a coaching client who believed he deserved a promotion. After he gathered his facts, we practiced, allowing him to find his authentic voice with clarity and certainty. In the end, he not only got his dream position, but also created a stronger belief in his own self-worth and power. Here are some guidelines to enhance your skills:

## Eight Guidelines to Powerfully Communicate Like A Pro:

1. **Be Clear with Yourself.** Ask yourself first, what is my truth in this situation? Is this what I truly think, or am I just trying to please someone else? Notice every time you use the word "should"— is it truly what you want or a different version of what you think you are supposed to do, say, think or feel? Learn to use discernment.

2. **Get Curious.** Ask provocative, interesting questions so you can learn as much as possible without it being an interrogation. Don't make assumptions by not asking. Try asking just one more question. And if you can't think of anything, ask, "Is there more?"

3. **Create Connection.** Speak from the heart. Encourage reciprocal communication so both parties have a chance to speak, be heard and honored. Learn about the other person and respect what's important to them. Use "I" statements, practice mirroring and have do-overs when needed.

4. **Listen Actively.** A conscious decision is made to listen with all of your senses, stay in the present moment and fully concentrate on what is being said (and not said) rather than just passively 'hearing' the message of the speaker. Active Listening works to understand the message and point of view of the speaker, gives verbal and non-verbal feedback and suspends judgment until hearing the complete message

5. **Ask for What You Want.** Not asking for what you want is an automatic no. Strive for concise and courageous communications. And if you do not get the desired outcome, do not take it personally. Do not allow your self-worth to change from rejection— no one can take away your self-esteem except you.

6. **Exude Confidence.** Build a strong internal sense of self and allow others see it. Speak with conviction and passion and be your own best advocate. Create credibility with direct eye contact, a strong handshake, verbal connections and being okay with silence. Practice being the expert and honing your skills with a friend or coach. And if you are scared, do it anyway.

7. **Take Responsibility.** Take responsibility for yourself and make your words count. Use your true voice clearly, confidently, respectfully and effectively. And please don't write an e-mail or text when a conversation by phone or in person is better. Show up and use your voice fully.

8. **Practice, Practice, Practice.** Practice speaking powerfully, directly, and graciously in as many life areas as possible. Use "I" statements and keep trying, keep going, fail, and show up again. Always do your best and recognize your successes.

The use of authentically communicating what you know, how you feel and what you need is one of the best assets I have discovered both personally and professionally. It is essential to use discernment, speak your truth, follow through with matched actions and show compassion and kindness to others. Lance Secretan was quoted in *Motto* Magazine by saying, "Authenticity is complete oneness in our thinking, speaking, feeling and doing. It's head, mouth, heart and feet all communicating and living the same message." So, speak your heartfelt truth because the world needs to hear what you have to say.

### Coaching Questions to Excavate Your Voice:

1. How are you using your voice to say what you need?

2. Notice every time you use the word "should." Is it truly what you want or a different version of what you think you are supposed to do, say, think or feel?

3. Make your words count by only speaking powerfully this week.

# Lead with Compassion

"To handle yourself, use your head; to
handle others, use your heart."
*Eleanor Roosevelt*

Many years ago, I believed leadership was all about strength, confidence, boldness, and always being strong, no matter what. I had the idea that leadership was authoritative and rising above it all. Messages like "Never let them see you sweat" prevailed, and I only thought people who had jobs or were community leaders were in a position of leadership. Even Spiritual Leader Mahatma Gandhi acknowledged by saying, "I suppose leadership at one time meant muscles; but today it means getting along with people."

This thinking remained true even when I was the President of the Junior League of Louisville in 2000-2001. I had received great training on how to run an organization and be a president, and I felt confident in that role. I was in a prominent leadership position leading an organization of over 1000 women, yet I was also fighting to save my marriage and keep my family intact after it had blown up only a few months before I took office. I compartmentalized, told no one and moved through it all with as much poise, determination and confidence as possible. The truth was... it almost killed me.

I painstakingly decided to move forward with a divorce after my term, resigned my remaining community volunteer roles and began my healing. I didn't think much about my impact, the role of leadership or anything else other than I needed to heal and find a way forward over the next couple of years. Then I became a Coach.

Coaching challenged me to come back to myself and step into my authenticity. After my initial training and a few years of practice as a Coach and a Speaker, I decided to take a 10-month leadership training for coaches in California. At the time, my hope was to take my business to the next level, and I achieved that by doubling my income in one year.

Yet, the bigger lesson was I learned about myself and what it meant to be a true leader. I discovered that everyone is leader, and it is not defined by titles, careers or roles. Leadership is about taking personal responsibility for your impact and using your influence for the greater good. It's about being conscious and clear about your passion, your purpose and how you want to show up in your home, your work and your community. It's about being the true you, being your best and asking for help when you need it. It's about showing compassion to others without sacrificing yourself, and allowing the emergence of vulnerability, truth, responsibility and being of service. As American Scholar Warren Bennis wrote, "Becoming a leader is synonymous with becoming yourself. It is precisely that simple and it is also that difficult." Below are my thoughts on being not only a great leader, but also bringing compassion, connection, creativity and success to your leadership abilities, no matter what your role is in life.

**15 Ways to Create Compassion, Connection & Success as a Leader:**

1. **Start with Self-Compassion.** In order to truly have compassion for others you must first have it for yourself. In other words, you can't give what you don't have. Practice self-care, gratitude and mindfulness.

2. **Invite Authenticity and Make it Personal.** Be your authentic best. Be real and make it safe for others to be themselves. Really get to really know others— who they are, what's important to them, their families and what they like to

do, personally and professionally. Live your values. Reveal your own emotions and be vulnerable because it creates connection and gives another person permission to do the same.

3. **Model Compassionate Leadership.** The best leaders lead from the heart, and know how to inspire others through kindness, respect, flexibility, trust, support and empowerment. Take responsibility for your personal impact. Show others how to be a good leader and that you care. You will create loyalty, job satisfaction and ultimately more success at work, at home and in your community.

4. **Offer Kindness.** Kindness is universal and has a huge impact. Even the smallest action such as a smile, a thoughtful note or "I believe in you" can break down barriers and create connection. Plus, it's good karma.

5. **Show Respect.** Let others be who they are. Honor someone's privacy. Don't gossip— it's their story to tell, not yours. Allow others to have their joy and pain, successes and failures.

6. **Use Conscious Communication.** Listen actively and be curious. Use, "Tell me more." Make eye contact, listen without interrupting, and acknowledge what the other person is saying to you. Self-manage by being aware of your own thoughts, words and actions; and choose your own words with mindful intent and integrity. Always let your words and actions meet.

7. **Be Honest.** People appreciate the truth, and candor is better than comfort, no matter what the news is. Forthrightness will build trust in the long run.

8. **Engage Empathy.** Try to understand and accept the perspective of the other person and put yourself in their shoes. "Find them right." Show genuine concern yet allow them to have their thoughts, feelings, beliefs, and above all, dignity. Do not try to take their pain away from them.

9. **Be of Service.** Be helpful, generous, offer guidance and pitch in when needed. Lend a hand to someone who is under stress, stuck or on a deadline. Ask, "How can I help?" Give the proper credit and remember that you are striving to meet the same goals and outcomes. Be encouraging and positive, not critical or undermining. And remember, true generosity expects nothing in return.

10. **Establish Clarity.** Set expectations in the beginning. Create accountability and make sure that you are clear about your goals, needs, and deadlines. The more you clarify things upfront, the better you can hold someone accountable. And add, "You have my support."

11. **Instill Inspiration.** Build in playdates and fun activities. Encourage learning through books, podcasts, trainings, continuing education and coaching.

12. **Encourage Creative Collaboration.** Recognize the synergy of people coming together to innovate, find creative solutions and possibly create something better together than alone. Ask, "What's working?" As a Coach, I believe everyone is "creative, resourceful and whole." Plus, contribution creates better buy-in.

13. **Give Positive Feedback.** Catch others doing it right. Acknowledge other people's strengths, attributes, wins and contributions— tell them and others often. Say, "I'm

proud of you." People need recognition and encouragement. When there is a problem, give feedback timely, directly and privately.

14. **Exude confidence.** Take charge, speak up, be strong, stay calm and be re-assuring when needed. Being compassionate is not weak, so maintain your conviction, clarity and confidence. Use your authority wisely. Be the leader you are meant to be.

15. **Recognize Our Common Humanity.** Show grace by understanding people will make mistakes. Practice forgiveness and understanding when needed. Say "I'm sorry" when appropriate. Find connection with others in the experience of life rather than being alienated by our own suffering.

Woodrow Wilson said, ""You are not here merely to make a living. You are here in order to enable the world to live more amply, with greater vision, with a finer spirit of hope and achievement. You are here to enrich the world, and you impoverish yourself if you forget the errand." I encourage you to consider the impact you have each and every day and remember the errand of your life.

**Coaching Questions to Inspire Leadership:**

1. Who are you as a Leader?

2. What intended impact do you want to have?

3. Given the above ideas, in what ways can you improve as a Leader? Practice each one until they are naturally integrated.

# Claim Your Success

*"Try not to become a man of success, but
rather try to become a man of value."*
Albert Einstein

Are you successful, and if so, in what ways? Are you happy with who you are and what you have achieved? Most often, success is defined by one's accomplishments—favorable endeavors that come to fruition; the attainment of wealth, position or honors; or a person who has achieved success. This description might be true for you, but I also believe the definition of success must include the "who you are" part, and everyone must create their own personal definition of success.

So, what does success mean to you? How do you define it, claim it and pursue it? Is it a plentiful bank account, a certain social status, the right home in the right neighborhood, a title at work or an educational degree? Is it your own happiness, the quality of your relationships or a balanced life? How do you know when you have made it to the top and truly arrived at your destination or reached your pinnacle?

Some people feel accomplished professionally. They have mastered their vocation, are recognized by their peers as an expert, have been rewarded financially and continue to find success in their work. Their self-esteem is tied to their career, yet other parts of their life may have suffered. Other people believe they have done well personally by taking care of their relationships, their health, their families–fulfilling the role of caretaker, yet carry a constant disappointment that they have not done enough, achieved enough or accumulated enough. Either way, success is being determined by what they do, not necessarily who they are as a person.

The key to success starts with creating your own personal definition of achievement that authentically aligns both worlds. Most people need a combination of both personal and professional victories, while maintaining life balance, personal connection, passionate pursuits, joyful accomplishments, service opportunities and true authenticity to one's life purpose and passionate pursuits.

The "being-ness" can be distinguished by your values, a strong sense of self, and seeing the good that already exists within you. It's the deserving, self-loving, joyful and happy you. The "doing-ness" can be defined by acknowledging what you have already accomplished and what you still have yet to do. Make a list of accomplishments, and really own what you have done and created— don't shrink small to your own greatness. Personal success is created by making choices that honor yourself and others while continually moving forward to reach your dreams and goals… and in the process, not betraying yourself along the way.

### What does it really take to be successful? Here are Five Keys:

1. **Passionate Determination** Success requires passion and determination. What excites you? Is there anything you are so bothered by that you have to do it? Get inspired, dream big, and don't accept less than you want or deserve. Envision your achievements and engage in creative solutions. What will make you relentless? "Success isn't a result of spontaneous combustion. You must set yourself on fire," said humorist Arnold Glasgow.

2. **Cultivated Clarity** Know what you want and why you want it. Know your why. What will you get when you get there? Intentionally create a clear vision by aligning

concise, pristine goals with your values and envision your achievements. Maximize your time, talent and resources. Be intentional. Decide what is right for you based on all life areas —emotionally, physically, mentally, financially, relationally and socially— and commit to your aspirations. British journalist David Frost said, "Don't aim for success if you want it; just do what you love and believe in, and it will come naturally."

3. **Confident Believability** Believe in your personal ability to succeed. Be fearless and adventurous--take risks and dare to succeed. Do you feel worthy? Do you believe in what you are doing? Embody your successful self and lead your efforts with self-confidence, fearlessness and unshakable certainty. Women's rights activist and novelist Lydia M. Child said, "Belief in oneself is one of the most important bricks in building any successful venture." If you do not believe in you, how can you expect others to do the same?

4. **Empowered Action** Artist Pablo Picasso said, "Action is the foundational key to all success." Put structures and systems in place. Take inspired action every day. Protect your goals, protect yourself from distractions. Choose 3 action items per day (that is 15/week, 60/month, etc....) Be grateful for your accomplishments and learn from your failures. And no matter what, keep moving forward. Do something, anything towards your goals and do not waste a moment not pursuing your dreams.

5. **Sustainable Self-Care & Support** Take extremely good care of yourself... you are your biggest asset. Learn what you need to do to work at your optimum level and get support. Put yourself on your calendar first and create a toolbox. — Self-care must be part of your business plan. Ask for help...

know when, know who and know how. Sometimes you need personal goals in order to achieve professional aspirations. And lastly, remember you are always in choice. As French philosopher Albert Camus said, "Life is the sum of all your choices."

The combination of "being" and "doing" is met with how you handle the ups and downs along the way. By doing the best you can in any given moment with the knowledge and resources on hand, you can build a strong foundation for continued success in any given situation. Here are some provocative inquiries to see if you are on your path to triumph.

## Thoughtful Coaching Questions to Move You Towards Success:

1. What does true success look like to you?

2. What kind of plan do you need to cultivate?

3. If your whole attention is focused on producing this result, what will you have to give up? Do you need to recalibrate and if so, where do you go from here?

4. What is your contribution to the world going to be? Is this your desired legacy?

# ENRICH YOUR
# RELATIONSHIPS

Do you feel full of connection and joy? Are you loved and supported in the world? In what ways? Do you like the company that you keep? Are you enjoying the people in your inner circle, or do you often feel frustrated with the behaviors and actions of those around you? If you are like many people, relationships can be difficult to navigate. They seem to bring the biggest joys as well as the toughest heartbreaks, no matter the type of relationship.

I know all too well the disappointments in relationships. When I divorced years ago, I not only lost my partner, but also many friends as a fall out of my new status. Suddenly I found myself re-thinking all of my connections, especially my social circles, and decided to get clear on who I wanted in my life and for what purpose. I realized I needed certain qualities in my relationships— such as love, support, loyalty, connection, reciprocity, depth and shared interests. I cleaned up my act, set boundaries, invested in and drew healthier, more aligned people into my world.

Relationships are defined in many ways— an exchange, association, rapport or involvement; an emotional connection between people. A tie to another. No matter what the connection, our relationships with each other are important. It is often said that the greatest desire for people is to simply love and be loved. I find that to be true, no matter if it's platonic or romantic love. I believe we all want to feel connected to others who can love us as we are. It is a human need to belong and to be wanted, cared for, desired, accepted and included— whether it's in our families, with our partners, with our friends, with our colleagues, within our community and even with ourselves.

All healthy, fulfilling relations need an investment of time and energy, including your relationship with yourself. It is important to make sure you are your authentic best by investing in your own growth. By having a strong self-worth, using effective communication tools, creating shared experiences, being spiritually rooted and taking personal responsibility in all of your encounters, you can create a strong foundation to better, more complementary relationships.

In my coaching practice, I assist my clients in finding true love within themselves, as well as attracting better connections with others into their lives. You can't control others, but having the right perspectives, boundaries, intentions and sense of self will allow you to improve all of your relationships in any given situation.

In this section, I share with you my tips for falling in love with yourself, cultivating your inner circle, knowing who's got your back, telling your truth, showing affection, sustaining love, keeping your side of the street clean and learning from your enemies. I also share my thoughts on soul sisters, creating your standards of integrity and transforming yourself and your relationships. There is no greater happiness than loving connections… let's get started enriching your relationships now.

# Fall in Love... Every Day

*"Each relationship you have with another person reflects the relationship you have with yourself."*
Alice Deville

Falling in love, being in love, staying in love... the wondrous state of loving someone and being loved in return. This experience is one of the greatest desires for most humans...the exhilaration, good feelings, and ecstatic joys that come with love. Yet, how do you bring this romantic love into your life with another person at the exact moment in time and then keep it alive? In other words, how do you get love, sustain love and evolve love?

Finding a person to love who also loves you back is not an easy task. As a Life Coach, I have had the privilege of witnessing many people's journeys to love, as well as the disappearance of love. Allowing one's self to authentically connect; be open and vulnerable with another person while maintaining a strong sense of self can be scary. It takes willingness, clarity, courage, faith, discernment and a strong belief that deep love exists no matter your current circumstances. But what happens when it seems love has faded or evaded you all together? What do you do when you so desperately want the euphoric feeling of being in love, but it just hasn't stayed or even found you yet?

I spent the decade of my 40's asking myself those exact questions, from both personal and professional perspectives, and I have created some strong opinions about the subject of romantic love. It is essential to believe in love, make the right choices and be really ready for the responsibility of a relationship. But more importantly, I believe attaining amorous love begins with you. You MUST love YOU first. Whether you are in a relationship, getting out of one, or desiring a new one, the first step is looking within and truly loving what you see and then sharing that beauty with another.

Source love from within and then you will have it to give to others freely. Don't get your deep happiness solely from another person and expect that person to fill in the pieces of yourself that feel incomplete. Love yourself as much as possible so you bring your best and most authentic you to another. After all, how can you expect someone to love you if you do not love, honor and respect yourself? Here are some suggestions for falling in love with yourself first.

### 14 Ways to Fall in Love with Yourself:

1. **Love yourself first.** Live your values in all life areas and embrace your awesomeness. Don't betray yourself in order to get others to like or approve of you. Determine your needs and try to meet some of them yourself.

2. **Become *really* interesting and interested.** Be curious. Take up a new interest, a fun hobby, a dream career, read more. Would you enjoy your company?

3. **Get inspired.** Learn something new. If you are adventurous, fill your life with adventures now. If you appreciate intellectual pursuits, join a book club or take a class now. If you love the arts, go to a museum, seek out a film festival, special art exhibit or play. Make plans and don't wait for someone, someday or something else to inspire you.

4. **Live a romantic life.** Add magic and sparkle... light candles, take bubble baths, eat chocolate, drink champagne, indulge in love stories, read poetry, dance, listen to music,

visualize. Create regular romance rituals that reflect how you want to feel.

5. **Feel good and look good.** Exude vitality. Take *extremely* good care of yourself. Let your inner beauty be reflected in your outward appearance. Refine your clothes, jewels, hair, and make-up. Live healthy and achieve your personal best body for you.

6. **Nurture your relationships.** Spend time with people you want to be with, not people you have to and really get to know them deeply. Look for your partner's soul through his/her eyes.

7. **Review your dating standards and don't go against yourself.** Know these, live these. For instance, one of mine was "Love him *as he is* or don't."

8. **Follow your heart.** Get out of your head, pay attention to your body. Let your head inform you, trust your intuition and listen to your heart... tap into all of your senses.

9. **Heal first.** Create clean closures and let go gracefully. Mend a broken heart so that you do not take baggage into your relationship. Clear out the clutter in your life so that *new* can come in. Deal with any past issues, don't play the "blame game," let go of old loves, failed relationships, disappointments or unmet expectations. Get rid of scorecards and don't hold others hostage to your past.

10. **Re-ignite your personal passion.** Grow and pursue your passions. Discover what makes you come *alive* and do that as much as possible. Dance, create, stargaze, exercise. Make love often.

11. **Love others compassionately.** Get outside of yourself. Give to others and make a positive impact on someone else—don't have tunnel vision for only this part of your life.

12. **Fill your own spiritual void.** Connect to the Divine, tap into your spiritual sources and have faith. Realize today's situation is not tomorrow's reality. Believe in love and trust that it will find you. Understand the higher purpose of a relationship.

13. **Be intentional and know what you really want.** Be clear about relationship dreams, desires and expectations. Do you want a soul mate? Companion? Caretaker? Have a BIG love, if that's what you want.

14. **Date yourself.** Take yourself out on dates and fall in love with the unique you. Go where you are celebrated. Make time for yourself and others.

As writer Mark Twain wrote, "Dance like nobody's watching; love like you've never been hurt. Sing like nobody's listening; live like it's heaven on earth." Fill up your life with love and let it flow everywhere…for yourself and others.

**Coaching Questions to Expand Self-Love:**

1. What is it to be generous with yourself?

2. Create your own…
   - Standards of Integrity: What's important to you? (See my "Manners Matter" chapter for a sample.)

- Rules of Engagement: How you are showing up, reflecting you, being in integrity and using discernment? In what ways might you engage?

3. Do something exciting *every day* that allows you to exude and attract love.

# Cultivate Your Inner Circle

*"Each friend represents a world in us, a world
possibly not born until they arrive, and it is only
by this meeting that a new world is born."*
Anais Nin

When you look at the company you are keeping lately, do you like what you see and how you feel? Is your cup being filled with connection, fun, joy and laughter? Are you being honored by the people around you and do your friendships have reciprocity?

Most people in life want to love and be loved, to see and be seen, to know and be known. Often their "knowingness" comes from their closest friends more than with anyone else in their world. Many people, especially women, long for a place to completely relax into themselves, to take off their masks, and to be accepted for who they really are. They want a place to go, not to be fixed, but simply to feel whole, safe and welcome… a home for their authentic selves.

Best friends can help create authentic, deeply connected, relatable relationships. These "soul sisters" provide a playground to experiment with different ways of being, to try out new things, to fully express feelings and emotions, to fail and start over, to speak their truth and to cultivate the person they are becoming. These close relationships often exhibit the qualities desired for other, sometimes more challenging, relationships with intimate partners, work colleagues or even family members.

As a coach, I have listened to many of my client's and friend's frustrations with the quality of their friendships. They have fallen into some bad habits such as not spending time with those important to them; holding on to friends who no longer work for them; not setting boundaries; not speaking up when needed; or even allowing others to decide who their friends are, rather than being proactive by choosing who they want in their inner circles. Many people are letting their friendships move to the bottom of the priority list, when it is precisely this camaraderie that makes them feel alive and nourishes them the most.

I believe there are only a handful of people who belong in our inner most circle. And these allies are not to be confused with our other relationships. For example, there are your "Archival" friends who have known you longest and bear witness to your life, and you always seem to pick up wherever you last left off. Your "Social" friends are your fun playmates who have common interests and provide fun and entertainment. Your "Work" friends are those you might spend a lot of time with due to work demands or volunteer projects, yet that might be the only thing you really have in common. "Circumstantial" friends help to bridge the gap, and give companionship when others are not available.

There is value in having friends in all of these areas, however, don't pick your alliances out of your circumstances such as work, community service, children's friends, neighbors or even your partner's spouses.

My suggestion is to choose and cultivate your inner circle—the relationships that enhance your soul for where you are in your life right now. Scottish Reverend and Professor Henry Drummond wrote, "Wherever we are, it is our friends who make our world." I believe it is best to pick close friends who align with your same values and beliefs. Begin by consciously designing a close circle of friends who will unconditionally support your life in all that you do and dream of doing. Here's how...

**Enhance Your Relationships by Honoring Your Values:**

Listed below are the more prevalent values I have unearthed with my coaching clients. I suggest you pick your top ten and rate them in order of importance to you and your needs for your closest friendships. And of course, feel free to add your own values. For a larger sampling, see "A Sampling of Values" in the Appendix.

| | |
|---|---|
| *Acknowledgement* | *Inspiration* |
| *Adventure* | *Integrity* |
| *Authenticity* | *Kindness* |
| *Beauty* | *Laughter* |
| *Belonging* | *Love* |
| *Collaboration* | *Loyalty* |
| *Compassion* | *Nature* |
| *Connectedness* | *Passion* |
| *Creativity* | *Peace* |
| *Empowerment* | *Personal Power* |
| *Freedom* | *Respect* |
| *Fun & Play* | *Spirituality* |
| *Growth & Learning* | *Strength* |
| *Harmony* | *Trust* |
| *Honesty* | *Validation* |

By knowing what is most important to you, you can choose to value yourself and revere those closest to you at the same time. Give yourself the freedom to open your heart and live your own values within your friendships. Consider who honors you with love, clarity, acceptance, support and reciprocity; and create the opportunity to grow and expand together through the challenges and joys on the journey of friendship.

**Coaching Questions to Evolve Your Relationships:**

1. Who is in your Inner Circle, and what do you want those relationships for?

2. When you leave the presence of another, do you feel better or worse? If better, then great. If worse, consider what changes might need to be made.

3. Who are "they" who hold so much power over you and your life?

4. What does it feel like to be truly loved, accepted and encouraged without judgment?

# Know Who's Got Your Back

*"Problems can become opportunities when
the right people come together."*
Robert Redford

Do you sometimes feel like you are all alone out in the world trying to make a difference? Do you think you have to do it all, or that you are the only one who can get things done, cares or can make an deep impact—whether it's a community project, work excellence, business expansion or even maintaining an orderly home? Do you find that in the process of doing and giving, you have become depleted, worn out, burned out and simply ineffective?

There is a misperception that successful people do it all. They seem to be independent superheroes who do everything with grace and ease, and still have a smile on their faces. The media, mentors, teachers and other well-intended people tell us in order to flourish, you have to work harder and keep going at all costs.

The truth is... the happiest and most successful people know they can't do it all and have built a life filled with an abundance of help and support from many different people. They know how to sustain their success because they balance their own roles with enlisting and receiving the aid of others. They understand who's got their back, create reciprocal relationships in which both people benefit and continually seek out supporters who align with their mission, passion and purpose.

No matter what your role is, being successful in your life requires leadership, confidence and discernment. In order to claim what you are best at doing, it is important to know when to delegate and recognize on whom you can count. Successful people are highly motivated, yet they realize they do not need to be the best at everything. They trust others, enlist advocates, let go of control, stay open to change, and know "done is sometimes better than perfect." Most importantly, they know how to build a stockpile of support for whatever they are trying to accomplish and are not afraid to boldly ask for it when needed.

My best example of this was my own decision to hire my assistant, Meredith, in the spring of 2006. I had started my Life Coaching business at the end of 2003, working only part-time so I could continue to prioritize my children's needs while they were young. As my business began to grow, I started to understand that if I wanted to expand my services, I would need help. I was scared to make the commitment, not knowing if I could really afford it. Yet, I knew I had to trust that hiring an assistant, along with having a coach, a mentor, creative collaborators and emotional supporters, was the next best step, and it was. Meredith does what she is best at by handling details, while it frees me up to do what I love and am best at doing, and that is inspiring sustainable change in others. Here is a coaching exercise to assist you in building a strong foundation and your ultimate pillars of support.

## A Coaching Exercise to Create Your Army of Advocates:

Who's got your back? Do you know who is truly there for you, and for what situations? Let the following coaching process will allow you to identify and create your best support system.

1. Make a list of your biggest fans and supporters.

2. Consider the various parts of your life, and think about who supports you in each of the following areas:
   • Personal

- Professional
- Emotional
- Spiritual
- Relationships
- Social/Cultural
- Financial
- Environmental
- Physical/Medical
- Community

3. Now consider anything with which you are struggling. What needs your attention the most?

4. Write down four people who can support you for each challenge. Where are you on the list?

5. Think about one thing each of these people can do to support you.

6. Consider any other ways you can get your needs met (hiring someone or asking a friend vs. doing it yourself.)

7. Now, decide and ask for what you need. People do not know what you truly want unless you make a genuine request. Remember, not asking is an automatic no.

8. Don't forget that relationships are reciprocal, so say thank you, pay on time and honor the people that assist you in being fabulous.

Having people who support you not only allows you to balance and expand yourself and your services but can also establish a more creative and synergistic collaboration that might not exist otherwise. Your army of advocates can ground you, inspire you, empathize with you, love you and pick you up when needed. The power of these interdependent connections will assist in your achievements and form life-long bonds that will make the journey much more pleasurable and fulfilling along the way.

# Soul Sisters

*"Oh soul, you worry too much. You have seen your own strength. You have seen your own beauty. You have seen your own golden wings. Of anything else, why do you worry? You are in truth the soul, of the soul, of the soul."*
Rumi

Soul sisters… the deeply connected females we believe know us best and love us the most. They are our closest friends who understand our essence, intuitively connect to our souls and withhold judgments by loving us no matter what. Many of us have close friends, but how many of them are truly, deeply, and madly your best girlfriend— a soul sister who has been to the depth of your despair and the height of your elation?

Our soul sisters embrace the beauty of our souls and reflect our goodness back to us. These mutually beneficial relationships can come from anywhere and during any life situation or cycle; but these connections almost always have a common experience and a shared sense of vulnerability. Soul sisters are often revealed during the pursuit of one's own mission of self-discovery when the two separate paths collide, and then they stick. So, how do you know if you have one, or for that matter, even need one?

As a woman and a life coach, I bear witness to my client's lives and their journeys that include their self-perspective, their challenges, their successes and the relationships that support them. I participate in their longing to be 100% authentically themselves while still being fully loved and accepted unconditionally. These women need a safe place to give and receive nurturance, as well as be able to unselfishly get their needs met with a caring confidant. It is that warm and inviting emotional support that allows intimacy to be created and a soulful relationship be born.

I am blessed in that I know I have at least three soul sisters with my natural sister Michelle, my best friend Valerie and my daughter Tess. Each of us has had enough pain, challenges, laughter, perseverance, strength and vulnerability to know we have that magical connection that cannot be severed. One of my favorite experiences is when Michelle and I go for walks and talk about life, the challenge of the moment, then the realization that there is an instant opportunity for transformation. With our creative spirits, learned perspectives and desire for knowing and understanding, we debate the meaning of life and our role in it. We can finish each other's thoughts and our synergy fuels us individually to go out and do what we do in the world.

Same with my best friend, Valerie, of the past 20 years. We can cry, laugh, create, complain; seek wisdom, guidance and understanding from each other; eat cookie dough and drink champagne— all at the same time. And with my daughter, Tess, we have a creative and spirited connection that intuitively understands the heart, provides honest feedback and laughs at the big and small things in life.

Our soul sisters provide a playground to experiment with different ways of being to try out new things, to fully express feelings and emotions, to fail and start over, to speak what is true and real and to cultivate the individual person we are becoming. Best friend relationships often exhibit the qualities desired in other, and sometimes more challenging, relationships with intimate partners, work colleagues or even family members. Don't get me wrong, I love my family and my friends— but my soul sisters just get me in a way that no one else does. They feed me, keep me clear, ground me, hold me up and push me forward, especially when I am not sure if I want to keep going. And, as we inspire each other, other people in our world benefit from this shared love. Here are some qualities to consider in finding and nurturing your soul sisters.

## Qualities of a Soul Sister and What You can do to Nurture One:

- **Authentic** so be real and your truest you.
- **Joyful** so be happy and laugh together often.
- **Truthful** so be open and honest.
- **Vulnerable** so deeply share pieces of yourself- successes and challenges, weaknesses and strengths, doubts and dreams.
- **Intuitive** so listen, internally and externally, more than you talk.
- **Connected** so have shared experiences.
- **Genuinely curious** so ask interesting questions and dig deep.
- **Heart-focused** not headstrong so be empathetic and emotional.
- **Empathetic** so experience the emotions together yet leave them behind when you part ways. Don't take away the other's pain.
- **Generous** so give and be of service.
- **Balanced** so reciprocate with each other.
- **Loyal** so be accountable and faithful to your commitments.
- **Caring** so be kind and supportive.
- **Strong** so take a stand for your beliefs.
- **Acceptance** so stop judging yourself and others.
- **Spiritually grounded** so spend time connecting to your Divine Source.
- **Present and available** so make time for the relationship and relish the experiences.
- **Optimistic** so see the good and be positive. Don't be a "Debbie downer."
- **Magically magnificent** so dream, create together and be each other's muse.

Let the soulfulness imbue and organically unfold. The connection will present itself if you show up fully and invest in your relationships. Define your sisterhood, co-create the relationship. Spend time together dreaming up cool possibilities for your lives and then support each other's separate journeys. Honor the other person's path and allow them to maintain their dignity, even when one person falls down or fails. Soul sisters instinctively know how to do this, always holding each other up strongly and treasuring the other's beautiful soul.

## A Coaching Exercise on Soul Sisterhood:

By knowing what is most important to you, you can choose to value yourself and revere those closest to you. Give yourself the freedom to open your heart with love and live your own values within your closest relationships. Create the opportunity to grow and expand your soul through the challenges and joys on the journey of your individual lives.

1. Who nurtures your soul?

2. Who do you strongly feel connected to? Do they share the same values and recognize your essence? Is there a spiritual connection?

3. How do your soul sisters support the evolving and growing you?

# Make Manners Matter

*"I seek constantly to improve my manners and graces,
for they are the sugar to which all are attracted."*
Og Mandino

Are you minding your manners? Are you saying "please" and "thank you;" sending hand-written thank you notes when people do something thoughtful for you; and being nice to the people around you? Are you being honorable, staying in integrity and being true to your word? I hope so because it seems to me that many people have either lost the art of etiquette or were never taught it. Having grown up in a southern state, I have a big appreciation for these small, but important, gestures of respect and kindness, and it concerns me that more people do not behave in a way that truly honors themselves and the people around them. This is a subject that I can really get on my soapbox and speak to anyone who will listen.

So, what is it about manners that are so important? Why do they matter so much, especially to us baby boomer southerners who hold these standards of polite behavior as ceremoniously sacred?

Many of us have grown up receiving guidance on how to behave— anything from "be nice on the playground, put your napkin in your lap, and say, 'please, thank you and you are welcome' to learning the Bible verse Luke 6:31, "Do to others as you would have them do to you." Other directives such as "treat others as you want to be treated," "honor thy mother and thy father," and my personal favorite, "we teach people how to treat us" live in our cells as we move through the world. These timeless nuggets of wisdom give us a code of social conduct, as well as a way to relate to others and navigate the world.

Yet, it sometimes seems that the whole manners thing can be about putting form over substance, especially if you are being nice to someone you do not like or are trying to get something from someone. After all, isn't it more important to be real and authentic, not fake or "putting on airs?" The truth is, having good manners is not really about the other person. It is about you and who you are as a person. What values you hold to be true, your self-image and how you feel about yourself; what kind of impact you want to have on other people around you; and how you are being your most authentic self in the world—these are the foundation for exhibiting genuinely good behavior.

Using good social graces is intended to reflect your own moral compass, as well as honor another person, not to be manipulative or get something from someone. It is not about the pretenses of doing the right thing, but rather it goes deeper than just following a prescribed set of rules. To me, manners aren't just about holding your fork the right way and doing the "should's" in life, but rather, having good manners represents how you feel about yourself by reflecting self-respect, as well as how you feel about others by showing loving kindness. Using the niceties in life implies a mutual respect for both yourself and the other person; and it opens the door for a more positive encounter and an opportunity for true connection. The truth is, using good manners builds trust and creates unity, and that is good for everybody.

As Etiquette Expert Emily Post said, "Manners are a sensitive awareness of the feelings of others. If you have that awareness, you have good manners, no matter what fork you use." When you extend kindness, you are saying to the recipient, "I see you" "You matter" and "I am curious about you as a person." Graciousness allows a present-moment connection to be made with another human being. And, when a spirit of generosity and compassion exists, your efforts can be reciprocated and shared. Below I have created my standards of integrity that can serve as a navigation system or guide to healthier relationships, more successful careers, higher social standing, and even inner peace... just let these manners truly reflect what's in your heart and soul, hopefully a loving kindness and respect for all human beings.

## Suggested Standards of Integrity to Live By:

- Smile don't frown.
- Be gracious and generous with yourself.
- Be considerate often by saying please, thank you and you are welcome.
- Generate fulfillment from within; don't depend on others for your own happiness.
- Care deeply, and don't be dismissive of others.
- Be present. No really, *be fully present* with others. This includes putting away electronics when you are with another person and giving up your relationship with your phone in order to have a relationship with a person.
- Get curious about others. Stop talking about you and ask about the other person. You already know what is going on in your life, so learn what's going on with another person. Don't be self-centered.
- Be brave by telling the truth in a way that is kind.
- Be compassionate and empathetic.
- Practice forgiveness, and don't hold grudges.
- Show respect to everyone.
- Clean up your language; don't use profanity or negativity.
- Create your own personal boundaries; don't forsake yourself or keep toxic people in your life.
- Stop being a victim by giving up complaining, criticizing or gossiping.
- Treat others as you want to be treated.

- Heal thyself first, and don't project your issues on another person.
- Cause no harm to others and take personal responsibility for your own impact.
- Write meaningful and heartfelt thank you notes, preferably by hand. What do you have to say to another that is loving, kind and soulful?
- Respect other cultures, their customs and rituals.
- Do something for another person without recognition or the expectation of receiving anything in return.

Irish novelist Laurence Sterne wrote, "Respect for ourselves guides our morals; respect for others guides our manners." If manners are a guideline for your personal behavior, then act accordingly. Here are some questions to assist you in integrating your truer self in the world.

## Coaching Questions for Authentic Manners:

1.  Who are you? What qualities do you possess?

2.  What is it to be integrity with yourself in the world?

3.  What is it to be generous and show kindness to others?

4.  How do you want to take responsibility for your impact in the world?

# Dare to Tell the Truth

*"If you don't tell the truth about yourself*
*you cannot tell it to other people."*
Virginia Woolf

Do you speak your truth? Do you openly reveal your own authenticity by letting others see the true you, or do shrink back not wanting to speak up for fear of rejection or disapproval? Do you sometimes stretch the truth ever so slightly, believing that the "little white lies" do not matter, when in fact; they make you feel terrible afterwards?

Telling the truth can sometimes be scary whether you are being who you are or using your voice to communicate your needs or observations. But if you do not speak up, what is the consequence of your own internal falsehood? Does the seemingly inconsequential bargaining of fudging the truth or staying quiet that internally takes place outweigh the hurtful voice of self-deception and dishonesty? When you go against yourself, your self-esteem starts to diminish. It is like playing a game by trying to make choices that will hopefully empower you, but if that becomes too scary, you then choose the path of least resistance that minimizes the pain and discomfort.

So, what does the truth really mean, and what makes it so hard? I remember playing the game, "Truth or Dare" as a teenager. A group of my friends would gather at the home of my childhood friend, Christine, and someone would suggest we play this game. Afraid of appearing foolish, I would anxiously ponder which choice to make as I paid close attention to the questions asked and dares made. I tried to figure out which one put me in the best light while creating the least amount of embarrassment. Afraid of what my friends would think, I usually chose the dare in lieu of not having to reveal anything too personal. I worried—would they still like me; would I be accepted; would I stay in the inner circle? Truth or Dare? Doing the dare was sometimes the easier solution, but I later learned that telling the truth by being vulnerable creates the intimacy, which has allowed those same friendships to still exist today.

Most people try to be forthright, but sometimes the whole truth is not revealed for fear of being judged, fear of not wanting to hurt another person's feelings or having to sit with the pain of shame for not being better, much less perfect. Daring to tell your truth frees you to live an authentic lifestyle without constrictions. Being honest about what is important to you and deciding how to reveal that to others is courageous, especially when they may not agree, endorse, approve or like it. But when you use your voice, it is a starting point for stronger relationships with yourself and others, or perhaps, a separation from those who do not know how to support you. By speaking YOUR truth, you sanction your own birthright to be happy and fulfilled based on how you want to impact the world around you. So, start telling the whole truth about yourself. One of my first mentor coaches, the late Cheryl Glassner would often say, "Tell the truth, and tell it quickly." I dare you to speak up now. Here's why.

## **Telling the Truth ...**

- Validates who you are and what you want.
- Invites you to be open, honest and vulnerable.
- Honors you and honors others.
- Asks you to stand up for yourself and for others to do the same.
- Insists you stop pleasing others.
- Frees other people from choosing for you.
- Alleviates anxiety and stress.

- Brings in the heart, not just the head.
- Opens the door to hear your inner wisdom or intuition.
- Sets you free from regrets, old behaviors and past patterns.
- Dismisses shame, co-dependency and negative self-talk.
- Teaches discernment and how to ask for the right help from others.
- Provokes personal growth and transformation.
- Imbues vitality, energy and empowerment.
- Makes decisions and clarifies the next step you must take.
- Builds self-confidence and self-worth.
- Ignites authentic action, propelling you towards your real goals and desires.

A Russian proverb states, "The bitter truth is better than a sweet lie." I believe the beauty in truth telling is that it allows dignity to be present through respect, honesty, and integrity— important qualities needed for true intimacy and authentic connection. I am not suggesting you give unsolicited opinions or cause harm with your language. Rather, I am an advocate of mastering discernment by looking inward at your intent, being thoughtful with your words and actions and understanding the impact you want to make on others. Another spiritual teacher, Brooke Jefferies used to say, "The truth is always good for you and the other (person)." Dare to share your truth with those around you today.

### A Daring Coaching Exercise around Truth:

Do you tell the truth to yourself first and then others? Do you trust yourself to make choices that are in your best interest? Let's shoot straight, defy any doubts and use courage in all that you say and do.

1. Answer the following questions truthfully:

   - Are you who you want to be?

- Do your words and actions meet?
- When do you allow yourself not to be your word? Are there any areas where "little white lies" or bargaining shows up?
- Do you feel strong physically, emotionally and spiritually?
- What needs are getting met? If some are not, what can you do to ensure that they do?

2.  Using your answers, dare to examine how truth shows up in all your life areas. Probe deeper to see if you are in integrity with who you are, what you do and how you engage in your relationships. Where do you need to be more forthright?

3.  Now, create a personal "Truth Telling Principles" list to guide you on your path of truth, and dare to tell the truth each and every day.

# Ah, Love, Sweet Love: The Sweetness of Romantic Love

*"Life has taught us that love does not consist in gazing at each other but in looking outward together in the same direction."*
Antoine de Saint-Exupéry

What makes life so sweet? As a coach I could share my thoughts on defining, creating, balancing and maintaining the many aspects of a sweet life. However, when I got to the heart of what I wanted to share, love emerged. Not just the universal, spiritual, higher consciousness, greater love for all mankind and the various relationships that make up our world, but the truly, deeply, madly romantic love and the criteria needed to sustain a healthy relationship. After all, when it comes down to what people want most in life, isn't it just to love and be loved?

So, what is love? How do you find it, keep and sustain it? And, why do so many people invest so much of themselves in looking for love? In her book *Finding True Love*, Daphne Rose Kingma defined love as "an experience of great emotional and spiritual awakening to the unbounded bliss that is the true condition of our souls. When we fall in love, we feel no separation between ourselves and the person we love or, for a time, from all others. It is the transcendent, luminous, lovely feeling of love that we desire most dearly, long for most passionately, and are filled by most deeply when it occurs in our lives. Love is a sanctuary for our spirits, a bath of empathy for our emotions, a tranquil meadow in which to nurture our fond hopes and dreams." Love makes us feel good, alive and purposeful, whether you are in a relationship, looking for one or choosing to be alone.

It is important to understand some basics to having amorous love, and it includes self-love, loving the other person and loving the relationship itself. Nourish and love yourself first and always be who you are; say what you feel and ask for what you need courageously; cherish your mate unconditionally; continually practice compassion and forgiveness; align your words and actions; treasure your relationship by celebrating, playing, remembering and honoring it; and show your love by making sure your words and actions match. Finally, practice three vital tools to sustain and grow your love... communicate consistently, co-create it by having a shared vision and deepen it with the passion that exists.

## My Top Three Tools for Sustaining Love in A Romantic Relationship:

1. **Communication** is essential for a successful relationship. Many relationships suffer from poor or little communication skills, so you need to gain the tools needed to share your feelings and to ask for what you need. Realize your partner's needs may not match yours, so talk about them. Disclose your thoughts, dreams, fears, hopes, wants, desires, opinions and anything else that comes to mind. Revealing your inner self creates intimacy, a deep bonding and a lasting connection. In *The Five Love Languages* developed by Gary Chapman, he identified the ways in which people feel loved: Physical Touch, Words of Affirmation, Quality Time, Acts of Service and Gifts. Do you know how you feel most loved, and what about your partner?

2. **Shared Vision** is about co-creating a life together. Do you know what direction you want to go, and does your partner want to go with you? For example, do you both

want children? Do you prefer to create a quiet life at home, or would you rather see the world together? Identifying your common interests and what goals you want to work toward will keep your relationship fresh, purposeful and on the same path.

3. **Passion** in romance sets apart your relationship from all others. What is it to love deeply and from the heart? When we have chemistry, a desire for our partner and the sexual expression of that, it creates a deeper connection and bond with the other person. What is pleasure? Learn about each other, be generous, take delight in each other's bodies and find the fervor, the zeal. It is easy to let the flame go out way too soon in a relationship, so discover ways to keep the fire burning.

## A Coaching Exercise to Enrich Your Romantic Relationship:

Are you the type of person with whom you would to spend the rest of your life? If so, you are ready for lasting love. An exercise I use with my Life Coaching clients when we work on their romantic relationship is a Wheel of Relationship that examines the level of joy in twelve major areas of their partnership; or if you are not in a relationship, the priorities you have for a partner. This process provides perspective, balance and focus on what is working and what might need attention. In each of these areas, rate your level of satisfaction on a scale of 1-10:

- Shared Goals/Vision & Creativity
- Communication & Conflict Resolution
- Love, Emotional Health & Happiness
- Career
- Money
- Sexual Expression & Physical Intimacy

- Family
- Celebrations, Rituals & Gifts
- Social Life & Friends
- Spirituality & Sacred Time
- Fun & Play
- Physical Spaces

To keep love alive and your relationship sweet, go for the kind, pure, raw, true, blissful, real love. In doing so, love can not only satisfy your soul, but also lead you back to your most authentic self. In this higher purpose, you can then reach your greatest potential and spread love to the rest of the world. Savor it, appreciate it, honor it and respect it... ah, love, sweet love.

# Show Your Affection

*"Too often we underestimate the power of a touch,
a smile, a kind word, a listening ear, an honest
accomplishment, or the smallest act of caring, all of
which have the potential to turn a life around."*
Leo Buscaglia

I admit it... I am a romantic at heart. I melt watching people hold hands, exchange sweet glances and give pecks to one another on the cheek. I enjoy seeing couples, young and old, honor their love by showing affection, warmth and kindness to each other. I somehow think it's a reflection of their deeper love by their willingness to reveal their fondness towards each other with a sweet sense of confidence, tenderness and devotion.

When it comes to exploring the topic of public display of affection, or rather "PDA", it seems to me that it can often be misinterpreted. On one hand, I believe in expressing love, embracing intimacy and connecting to your partner in a way that honors not only the individuals but also the relationship itself. Yet, PDA has earned a bad reputation too often when some people cross a line, allow their displays to be inappropriate and do not respect boundaries, theirs and others.

Let's consider the importance of affection. For couples, it can be an expression of love and serves as a reminder to each other that they are connected. For others, it can be sweet gesture that reunites, welcomes or greets someone with respect, kindness and caring. Some people meet their friends and family members with a hug or quick kiss. Consider the customs of individuals in other cultures who perhaps give a kiss on one or both cheeks. Even with strangers, a smile is shared, and a hand is extended to someone you first meet, thereby showing affection immediately. The right physical touch, whether in an intimate relationship or new introduction, can create a safe connection, a trusted bond, and the good, warm feelings that are so often desired.

So, what keeps you from fully expressing your own feelings and affections towards others? Do you have an open heart not only to your partner but also others in general? Are you comfortable in your own skin and feel confident about the person you are presenting to the world? If not, you must first feel good about yourself in order to show your affection genuinely and lovingly towards others. Here are some tips for creating a closeness that will allow affection to be present.

## **Tips for Creating Affection and Intimacy in Your Relationships:**

- Nourish and love yourself first.
- Always be who you are.
- Look good, feel good and be healthy.
- Have impeccable hygiene.
- Cherish your mate unconditionally.
- Love deeply.
- Be generous with others.
- Treasure your relationships.
- Disclose your thoughts, dreams, fears, hopes, wants, desires.
- Say what you feel.
- Smile all day.
- Ask for what you need courageously.
- Continually practice compassion and forgiveness.
- Align your words and actions.
- Have an open heart.
- Don't withhold affection as punishment.

- Learn about each other.
- Meet strangers with a handshake.
- Give hugs freely.
- Extend graciousness and kindness always.
- Communicate consistently.
- Know your boundaries.
- Deepen your passion.
- Be bold.
- Reveal your inner self.

When you feel good and share yourself with others, a natural friendliness and liking can be extended in all of your relationships. Learning to show affection in a way that is right for you can not only satisfy your soul but also lead you back to your most authentic self. In this higher purpose, you can open your heart, share your uniqueness and spread love to others. Smile, hug, kiss, hold hands, and love as much as possible.

### A Coaching Exercise to Show Your Affection:

How do you show affection in the world?

- With your romantic partner, how do you keep the chemistry alive?
- With your family, how could your affections break down any barriers and create stronger bonds? How do you express love towards them?
- With friends, how do you want to honor them with your affections?
- With new acquaintances, how could a sign of warmth or smile facilitate a new relationship?

# Keep Your Side of the Street Clean

*"Turn your wounds into wisdom."*
Oprah Winfrey

Do you sometimes find yourself in messy situations, wondering how to best navigate the clean-up? Do you sometimes get your feelings hurt, only to remain quiet and later feel down or even resentful? If so, you are not alone.

In my coaching practice, I witness people who have a difficult time clearing up their life situations and have become either disenchanted or dis-empowered. Their distraught has been created for various reasons, and it seems the longer they wait to clean it up, the more difficult it can become to fix it. From misunderstandings, a lack of clear communication, made-up assumptions and stories, fear of hurt, disappointment or disapproval to victimization, self-imposed shame, guilt or anger, and a lack of self-esteem or confidence, they often sacrifice their own self-worth by trying to keep peace. And, without having the right tools or support to address it, they avoid confrontation and the situation can become irreparable.

This topic reminds of one of my fondest childhood memories of making mud pies at my grandparent's house. My sister and I loved getting our hands dirty and making beautiful creations with the ingredients of nature. We spent hours playing outside knowing it was okay to get soiled and be messy. No matter how filthy our hands, faces, clothes and work areas would get, we understood that we had to clean it all up before dinner and our parents' pick-up time. Although my grandmother, Mema, would work her magic in freshening us up (she always had a hot bath waiting for us), we still had to be responsible for our carefree afternoon of messiness by cleaning up as much as we could on our own.

What I love about this story is the importance of having fun in life, and realizing there can be much playfulness, fun and creativity in getting down in the dirt. Those timeless afternoons provided a great sense of fun and freedom as well as a great reminder that although being grubby and carefree instills creative playtime and rich experiences, it is still necessary to clean up the disarray before you can go on to what is next. For instance, it is important not to take hurt or disappoint into the next relationship or create false expectations in the next job just because you had a bad boss in this one. And if you make a mistake or offend another person, learn to ask forgiveness.

Life is messy, and what often starts off as a good intention or connected relationship can sometimes turn bad. I am glad there is the freedom to risk participating in new endeavors; to choose free will; to try something new and fail; and to immerse into chaos and confusion with people, places and situations. The result can be enormous personal growth and new passionate ventures. Yet, I also believe that there needs to be personal integrity, a relinquishing of the ego and a willingness to be accountable for one's role in any given situation. You cannot let things get messy without being willing to clean up your part, big or small.

I believe most people are good at heart, and they are doing the best they can under the stresses and challenges of the world today. People are not perfect, mistakes are made. Yet, many people can do a better job of "keeping their side of the street clean" by learning to take responsibility for their decisions, feelings, actions, words and the impact they have with other each other. Here are some tips on tidying up.

## Tips for Keeping Your Side of the Street Clean:

- Admit when you are wrong and learn to apologize gracefully.
- Be honest with yourself and others.
- Have integrity by doing what you say you are going to do.
- Take responsibility for your own emotions.
- Consider all perspectives.
- Treat others as you want to be treated.
- Tell the truth and tell it quickly.
- Always be kind.
- Set boundaries and learn to say no.
- Don't try to control, fix or change others.
- Choose happiness over being right.
- Speak up: ask for what you want and don't be a doormat.
- Don't take shortcuts or be passive-aggressive.
- Cause no harm to yourself or others.
- Don't gossip.
- Don't keep repeating the same mistakes.
- Forgive and ask for forgiveness often.
- Understand the power of your personal impact.

Learn to be comfortable with making messes. Choose happiness and joy, forgiveness and compassion, openness and discernment. Say yes to you and no to the bad behavior of others. Try new things and risk failing. And, when you unintentionally cause harm to another person or make a mess of a situation, admit your shortcomings, ask for forgiveness and learn to clean up after yourself along the way.

## Coaching Questions to Clean it Up:

1. Is there a current mess in your life you have been unwilling to look at or take action to clear? If so, what bold step can you take to move through the fear?

2. Who is making you mad, and what are you willing to do to make those relationships different? What are you tolerating? Where do you need to look at your behavior, or perhaps let go? Do you need to admit you are wrong or say you are sorry?

3. From the list above, choose one new helpful tool each week and practice integrating it into your life.

# Our Unlikely Teachers: Learn from Your Enemies

*"Whenever you are confronted with an opponent. Conquer him with love."*
Mahatma Gandhi

How do you deal with difficult people in your life? Do you confront your anger and speak up about your hurtfulness, or do you silently retreat, finding reasons to distance or no longer like them? Are you quick to judge, or do you take a moment to gather all necessary information? Do you actually have a nemesis, in other words, an opponent or rival whom you cannot overcome, and if so, how does that affect your life?

Having a difficult person or enemy in one's life can be frustrating and even heart-breaking. It can create harm to many people and take up a great deal of energy, sometimes resulting in the decision to create frenemies. After all, the saying "Keep your friends close, and your enemies closer" has been a long-time mantra for many people.

In researching the meaning and origin behind this quote, I discovered this statement was used as a strategic perspective on how to get ahead. "Keep your friends close, and your enemies closer" has been attributed to many sources such as the Chinese General and Military Strategist Sun Tzu or even the from the popular 1974 movie, *The Godfather Part II*, in which Michael Corleone stated this as a lesson from his father Vito. The most likely source I could find points to Niccolò Machiavelli's work, *The Prince,* which describes how to be a dictator.

In more modern times, I have observed people using this phrase to have the advantage in any situation and to remind themselves and others that they need to stay alert and protect themselves out of fear of being hurt, betrayed, left behind or kept in the dark. One might think it is important to know your enemies so that you can stay a step ahead or be ready for the unknown or an attack. Yet it seems to me that this perspective is somewhat unproductive; can create much drama, wasted energy and lost time; comes out of fear, paranoia and distrust; and does not instill faith, trust and certainty. I believe there is something to learn from every experience and every person who comes into one's path, especially those people who are more difficult— they can be our greatest teachers.

So, what if you replace the energy of worrying about the negativity that might be ensuing from an unfriendly foe and instead look at the potential learning? What if you could take a difficult situation or a challenging relationship and consider what there is to garner from the experience? And what if the people who are most difficult in your life are showing you an area in which you can grow into a better person?

Keep your enemies close not to get ahead, but instead, to move forward by growing yourself. When difficulty arises, I suggest you turn towards your so-called enemies, or the people in your life who are difficult or hard to get along with and make some observations. For instance, perhaps there is an opportunity to learn more about this person, their struggles and your lesson is to show kindness or compassion. Is this person showing you something within yourself that you might need to change? For example, maybe there is someone who is judgmental. If so, where in your life are you harsh, quick to judge or unfairly opinionated? And to take it one step further, is this person serving as a mirror for something you don't like about yourself? For example, do you find yourself irritated by people who are lazy, selfish or rude? If so, maybe there is an area in your life where you are lazy, selfish, or rude— or perhaps they are serving as a reminder to be diligent, selfless and courteous.

Just to clarify, sometimes the lessons are not always about seeing your weaknesses, but rather there is a need to set boundaries with people who drain you, harm you or treat you poorly. There are people who are just downright mean, insecure and they do not play fair. Even then, the lesson is to say no, and realize that you deserve to have people in your life who treat you with dignity and respect. After all, we teach people how to treat us. Here are some additional thoughts on dealing with difficult people or situations.

## Top 10 Questions to Ask Yourself in Dealing with Difficulty:

- What is the situation?
- Is this real or made-up?
- What is difficult, challenging or uneasy about this for me?
- What is their part?
- What is my part? How do I keep the focus on myself?
- Is this person showing me something I want to change about my behavior?
- What is my learning or lesson?
- Who do I want to be in this situation?
- What do I want to do about it? Do I need to make an amends, build a bridge, show kindness, confront, learn more, ask for help, set a boundary, ignore, or walk away?
- What's next? How do I want to take respectful, loving and productive action?

On a final note, I believe our enemies not only give us the opportunity to learn our lessons, but also to grow our heart and soul through compassion. Poet Henry Wadsworth Longfellow wrote, "If we could read the secret history of our enemies, we should find in each man's life sorrow and suffering enough to disarm all hostility." Spiritual Leader Mahatma Ghandi said, "Whenever you are confronted with an opponent, conquer him with love." By extending the gift of love, kindness and respect to the people who are most difficult to love, our own capacity to love deeply expands. And finally, British novelist Phyllis Bottome wrote, "There are two ways of meeting difficulties: You alter the difficulties, or you alter yourself to meet them." Which will you choose?

## Some Coaching Questions to Consider:

1. Is there currently someone or something in your life that exists to teach you something?

2. What can you do with the negativity in your life in order to grow? Is a boundary needed?

3. Where can you extend more love and compassion to others in your life? (Don't forget to include yourself.)

# BREAK FREE

W hat makes a person feel free? What is it to be powerful, strong and full of choices? What would it look like to reach your full potential matched with your deepest dreams and desires? If you are like most people, you desperately want to attain your goals, but often get sidetracked by the demands and expectations of others or even your own internal voices.

Freedom can mean different things to different people. For some, it's the freedom to be who they are or the freedom to express themselves without negative repercussions. Others define freedom financially or the ability to move about the world freely. And for some, freedom comes in the form of less stress, worry or fear. For me, I have experienced the need to overcome the lack of freedom in many of these areas, so I know it's possible to break free from whatever holds you hostage.

Wherever you are in your journey, breaking free is about releasing yourself from whatever holds you back from being your true self. It's ridding yourself from past choices or disappointments and moving in a direction that embraces all that you want for your life. It's about letting go of shame, guilt and regrets, and instead, choosing positivity, empowerment and real freedom.

As a coach, one of the most difficult things for my clients is to deeply believe in getting what they desire. Their fractured thinking and doubts can be far from wholesome certainty. They often come to me with fears, negativity or limiting beliefs, and one of the things we work on is to turn those limitations into empowering thoughts, inspiring actions and belief in themselves and what they are doing. ... and keep them on that path. They learn that they are entirely enough, incredibly deserving, creatively resourceful and genuinely empowered.

In this final section of *The True You Reimagined*, I hope that you will find the final tools you need to assist you in becoming your best you. It's the final frontier, the last piece of the puzzle, the juicy details that will allow you to transform those final aspects of yourself that keep you from what you desire. From accessing your personal power, freeing yourself, letting go of regrets, embracing your emotions, making powerful choices, going with the flow to making space, creating boundaries, owning failure, taking responsibility and going beyond illusions— there is something to help break down the barriers and remove the personal shackles in order to reach your full potential.

My wish for you is that you will live a full, rich life unencumbered by internal or external problems that arise. I hope that your challenges will become transformational opportunities, a place to learn and grow from anything and everything. You are the sum accumulation of all of your experiences. So, let's show the world what a powerfully authentic person you are and what it looks like to become "the true you reimagined."

# Access Your Personal Power

*"You were born with potential.*
*You were born with goodness and trust.*
*You were born with ideals and dreams.*
*You were born with greatness.*
*You were born with wings.*
*You were not meant for crawling, so don't.*
*You have wings.*
*Learn to use them and fly."*
Rumi

What makes a person powerful? Is it their money, fame, position, charisma, social status or expertise? Some of these things are important, but the most powerful person has the ability to use not only their external resources, but also access and activate their internal gifts and talents. An influential person is first and foremost true to themselves, and their internal make-up is reflected in their outside world of relationships, work, community and environment. Are you using your powers for good?

Powerful people put their stake in the ground on what they know to be their truth and continue moving toward the greater good of self and others. The leadership in their own lives becomes intoxicating to those around them, and they can't help but naturally empower others. Their authentic power is apparent, and their intense presence is aligned with their own personal values, continual personal growth and resulting external actions.

Do you feel powerful in your life and if not, why? Maybe you are not tapping into all of your greatest assets or fully using your potential. Perhaps you are still living the "life scripts" someone else gave you or you have forgotten the dreams and aspirations you once had. Maybe you have given your power away to someone who emotionally or financially supports you, but does not truly listen, understand or even know you.

No matter where you are in your life, I believe you can regain your power by taking small steps to access that forgotten energy. After all, your personal power is not something you get from things or others, it is something that already exists within yourself. You just have to remember where it is and then retrieve it.

**12 Ways to Access Your Authentic Power:**

1. The Power of **Self** Know you and your values, what is important to you and your limitations. Claim your own personal power, as opposed to letting others define you. Identify your own personal power.

2. The Power of **Passion** Know what makes you come alive and pursue those activities that help you feel connected to yourself, others and your community. Give yourself permission to engage in your playful pursuits often. And if you do not know, think about what makes you mad in the world and that might give you some insight about other possible hidden passions.

3. The Power of **Expansion** Keep learning and being curious. Dream, visualize, grow and create. The sky is the limit and there are unlimited possibilities and resources surrounding you.

4. The Power of **Intention** Decide what you want and be fierce for it. Use powerful thoughts, words and actions to support your vision create meaningful influence and purposeful impact.

5. <u>The Power of **Connection**</u> Share your dreams with others who will support your ideas and visions. Engage in creative collaboration. Connect to the power sources and people who feed your soul— loyal advocates, a Higher Power, mentors, coaches, supportive friends and close family members.

6. <u>The Power of **Choice**</u> You are always in choice about your thoughts, beliefs, feelings, attitudes and actions. Choose who you want to be and who you show up in the world. Be real and set appropriate boundaries when needed.

7. <u>The Power of **Words**</u> The permanence of language can be used to motivate, inspire and build up. Or it can be hurtful, harmful and used to tear down. Listen actively and say what you need to say. Learn to say no when you mean no and yes when you mean yes. Communicate clearly, positively and responsibly.

8. <u>The Power of **Action**</u> A great idea without action is simply an idea. Do something, anything, to make it real. Move, dance, go outside, make a phone call, set up a meeting. Be proactive, not reactive, and get going. You only need to take the next best step, every step of the way.

9. <u>The Power of **Risk**</u> Take a chance on changing and being uncomfortable, unpopular or scared. Be bold and fierce in pursuit of what you believe to be true. Be afraid and do something anyway.

10. <u>The Power of **Giving**</u> Give your time, talent, energy and resources to others without expecting recognition or sacrificing yourself. Financial expert Suze Orman says, "Generosity must be good for you and the other." Tithe.

Be charitable, generous, kind, compassionate, and brighten someone else's day as often as possible.

11. <u>The Power of **Faith**</u> Let go and trust in God, a Higher Power, or the Universe, as well as yourself. Exercise faith by deeply trusting, believing and acting in alignment with your beliefs, dreams and desires. Let go of fear, anxiety and control. Act as if what you want already exists.

12. <u>The Power of **Wisdom**</u> Be the expert of your life and use your experiences, your intuition and your wisdom to serve others. Never go against yourself and don't be afraid to speak up and share what you know and believe to be right.

It is within your power to become as happy, content and successful as you make up your mind to be. Accessing your personal power will create the self-confidence you need to take the necessary actions to ensure your desires come to fruition. By unleashing your power within each of these areas, you can go from feeling powerless to being powerful each and every day.

## **Powerful Coaching Questions:**

1. What is it to be powerful?

2. What qualities do you possess that will make you more able to reach your full vitality?

3. Are there any people, circumstances or beliefs to which you give away your power? If so, how can you change course?

4. In what ways can you expand your own power base?

# Free Yourself

*"We must be free not because we claim
freedom, but because we practice it."*
William Faulkner

What makes a person free? I often think about what freedom actually means and am grateful we live in a country that was founded on the basis of individual freedoms, liberty for all, limitless opportunities and advantageous privileges. Yet, as individuals, I observe many people who do not feel free within the lives they have created. Sometimes they feel locked into their circumstances, restricted by their choices, and are scared to even question their lives, much less make changes.

But what if you could feel free to start living the life you are really meant to live? Have you ever thought about what it would be like to have complete and utter freedom? Do you know what freedom really means to you? I have come to realize that "freedom" carries many different meanings for different people. For some, it is the freedom to be who you are, or the freedom to express yourself fully without holding back and worrying about the consequences. Others define freedom financially according to their pocketbooks, believing money gives them more choices. Freedom can also be defined as the ability to come and go as your please—to travel and to explore the world. And, freedom can also be defined by the ability to learn about yourself, to connect to others and to love whomever you choose.

Another way to think about having freedom is by making

choices *within* the life you have already created. For example, being able to have a job you love as opposed to the one that brings in the paycheck or being able to do something for yourself without guilt if the primary focus has always been on helping others. Or even having the ability to pursue other interests or hobbies, without always feeling like there is not enough time, money, energy or opportunity to engage in what you want, much less enjoy it.

I believe freedom is about knowing that you have choices, no matter what the circumstances. No one can take away your thoughts, feelings, beliefs, attitudes, dreams or perspectives. You have the autonomy to believe what you do, think what you want and feel what you feel without any restrictions. It is your free will and human right.

I hear people say, "I don't have a choice." It might be true there are certain responsibilities, restrictions, commitments or situations that might need to be honored, or something has been handed to you that you might not have preferred. Yet, I believe you can choose your perspective on a situation, dream of new possibilities and start making decisions to see things in a different light or do something in a new and different way. You can move toward a life with more freedom.

## Ways to Find Your Freedom:

What holds you back? What are the thoughts, the stories you make up, the boxes you put yourself into that hold you back and keep you from being authentic? What do you need to let go of in order to move toward more freedoms in all aspects of your life?

*"The Let Go's"*

- Freedom to Let Go
- Freedom from Stress, Worry and Anxiety
- Freedom from "Should's"

- Freedom from Low Self-Esteem or Self-Deprecation
- Freedom from Negativity
- Freedom from Being Defensive
- Freedom to Make Mistakes and Start Over
- Freedom from Fear
- Freedom from Doubt
- Freedom from Shame & Guilt
- Freedom to Cut Loose
- Freedom from Past Disappointments
- Freedom from Unrealized Dreams or Goals
- Freedom from Conformity
- Freedom from Disconnecting, Disassociating and Unavailability

*"The Move Towards"*

- Freedom of Choice
- Freedom to be Who You Are
- Freedom to Love
- Freedom of Expression
- Freedom of Self-Confidence
- Freedom to Explore
- Financial Freedom
- Freedom of Learning and Knowledge
- Freedom of Our Own Thoughts, Feelings and Emotions
- Freedom to Take Action
- Freedom of Acceptance and Peace
- Freedom of Human Rights
- Freedom to Speak Up
- Freedom of Connection
- Spiritual Freedom

It is within your power to become free and fulfilled. You might not be able to make immediate changes in your life at this moment, but you can start dreaming and working towards something new. Better yet, you can free yourself by changing the viewpoint or perspective you currently hold. After all, you are as joyful as you decide to be, and you can start now.

## A Coaching Exercise to Free Yourself:

1. Using the list above, define what freedom means to you.

2. What do you need to free yourself from, and in what areas of life do you need relief?

3. What will liberate you?

4. Once you have discovered of what you need to let go, you will have the freedom to go toward something new. What will you choose?

# Do-Overs: Let Go of Regrets

*"Regrets are as personal as fingerprints."*
Margaret Culkin Benning

Ever wish you could do "it" over? Live in another home, city or country; drive a different car or make an out-of-the-ordinary purchase; study something else or pursue an alternative career? Do you wish you married your first love, or put more effort into a friendship that ended? Do you spend your time on a daily basis thinking about what you could have said or done to comfort a loved one but didn't; overreacted by yelling or saying something you did not mean; or perhaps, you were not clear about how you responded to someone, regret the things you said or didn't say and are constantly replaying it in your head?

The regrets in your life can keep you stuck. These misgivings can build up to where they weigh you down, and, over time, the more weighed down you are, the more difficult it becomes to move forward. So, what qualms still plague your mind? What decisions or lack thereof still haunt you? What unfilled dreams and desires still exist? The keys to taking the load off and starting fresh are to relinquish your past mistakes and disappointments, to let go of guilt and sadness, and to forgive yourself, and then change your perspective and create a new definition of happiness. And, when necessary, have a do-over to clear the pathways to fulfillment.

Do-overs can take the form of changing a specific aspect of your life or even going back to someone to make a simple apology. Lost time can never be recovered, and your words or actions can never be completely taken back once they have been delivered. You might unintentionally hurt someone's feelings, not show your appreciation or inadvertently disappoint another; yet, you can make amends and change current behaviors into more loving connections.

On a more positive side, Henry David Thoreau wrote. "Make the most of your regrets; never smother your sorrow but tend and cherish it till it comes to have a separate and integral interest. To regret deeply is to live afresh." I believe do-overs give you the chance to start fresh and discover what you truly want at any given point in your life. A do-over can ignite dreams unfilled, re-connect you to people you miss and grow you as an individual. They provide learning opportunities to create more inner peace and harmony in your relationships and design the experiences in life you will truly treasure. Here are some guidelines on knowing when you need a redo.

## A Do-over is Needed When...

- it allows you to learn more about who you are and what is important to you.
- your own dreams and desires become crystal clear, and you now need to take a different path.
- you need to apologize or make an amends to another person, except when it will cause additional harm.
- forgiveness and compassion are more important than being right.
- it allows you to face a re-occurring fear and diminish its hold on you.
- you change your mind or decide to go a different direction and it impacts others.
- you want to invest in making a relationship stronger.
- it teaches you to be open, honest and vulnerable in order to create intimacy.
- you need to set boundaries for future healthier interactions.

- you learn new information that changes a current perspective or viewpoint.
- it allows you to practice speaking your truth and therefore build more self-confidence.
- you need to pivot and are ready for a new beginning or fresh start.

A do-over can enhance your confidence, and perhaps even open the door to receive something you may not have been truly ready for in the past. As Don Miguel Ruiz wrote, "Always do your best. Your best is going to change from moment to moment; it will be different when you are healthy as opposed to when you are sick. Under any circumstance, simply do your best, and you will avoid self-judgement, self-abuse and regret." A life full of conscious, proactive choices and always doing your best can turn our biggest regrets into our greatest adventures. I hope you will get started now.

## Coaching Steps to Turn Around Your Biggest Regrets:

Do you let yesterday's regrets use up too much of today's opportunities? What will you do to change that for yourself?

1. Make a list of your deepest, biggest regrets.

2. Are there items on the list that you still desire and want to pursue; or perhaps, is it time to let go of past disappointments or unfulfilled wants?

3. What is the opportunity now?

4. Focus on the positives instead of the "what ifs." Create a new vision of what you want and decide what steps you will take to get that for yourself.

# Make Powerful Choices

*"Don't ask yourself what the world needs. Ask yourself what makes you come alive, and go do that, because what the world needs is people who come alive."*
Gil Bailie

What makes you feel good? The fleeting moments, the guilty pleasures, the favorite activities, the silly amusements, the little indulgences? There are many things that you can do to make yourself *feel* better in the moment. Sometimes those things are only temporary or fleeting and other times they are a part of us and feed our souls. But what if those things stop working? What do you do next?

Doing things that makes us feel good are important and it helps us to understand our authentic preferences. It also fuels our desire to create more positivity in our lives. Yet, you must couple that with your inner truth and make conscious choices. Are you fulfilling your soul's deepest longing and purpose? If your answer is no, why not? Feeling good is a choice and knowing and believing you have options. Nothing feels better than the freedom to choose what is right for you, to be empowered, to exercise your free will and to let your inner beauty shine through.

People come to me who have become disenchanted by life circumstances or disempowered by others based on misunderstandings, lack of communication, financial dependence, seeking approval, trying to keep peace, or not wanting to hurt or disappoint another person. They have become the sum of their life choices, yet they keep making the same mistakes.

I often hear people say, "I don't have a choice." Yet, I believe you do. You get to decide how you show up in the world. Your current circumstances may not allow you to do and get everything you want now, but you can certainly begin to create what is next and make a new plan. In every moment, you are in choice with your thoughts, your feelings, your beliefs, your attitudes and your actions— those are yours and cannot be taken away.

Coaching can help you understand what will ultimately fulfill you, as well as give you the permission, the tools, the communication skills and the freedom to start moving your life forward. The process allows you to create powerful choices and actions based on who and what you want to be, how you want to do something, who you want to do it with and when you want to get started. Choosing an old pattern or behavior can make you feel bad and it denies you the opportunity for transformation and growth. Unless you start exercising your freedom of choice and basking in the beauty that awaits you, you will remain imprisoned, believing you have little control over your destiny or dreams.

### **Eight Tips for Making Strong Choices:**

1. **Be Honest with Yourself** Are you feeling good about where you are in your life and who you have evolved into? Are you living the life you truly want to experience?

2. **Keep Your Integrity** Don't let someone else's attitudes become yours if they do not ring true for you. What do *you* think? Make your actions and words meet.

3. **Let It Be** Don't control, fix or try to change others. Keep the focus on you.

4. **Set Boundaries and Learn to Say No** Create clear boundaries with yourself and others. And remember, what others think of you is not your concern.

5. **Change Your Mind** You have the right to make a different choice based on new information and situations.

6. **Use Your Voice** Speak up and ask for what you want. Don't be a doormat or let anyone run over you.

7. **Self-Care is Critical** Make self-care part of your life/business plan. Deal with stress by creating a toolbox to counter the impact. Get your needs met and take time to stay grounded and relaxed.

8. **Be Grateful for What You Have in Every Moment** Create a list of everything for which you are thankful.

Choose happiness and joy, purpose and passion, forgiveness and compassion. Examine the energy and impact of people, places and things that currently exist in your life— the good for you versus the bad for you. Choose the good, say yes to you and no to the bad behavior of others. Choose to live your values and align your choices accordingly. Choose to live a life that is fruitful, abundant and completely used up in the end. Commit to living your deepest dreams and desires, moment-by-moment, step-by-step... one choice at a time.

**Coaching Questions to Get Empowered Around Your Choices:**

1. Are you being nice or are you being real?

2.  Notice every time you use the word "should." Is it truly what you want or a different version of what you think you are supposed to do, say, think or feel?

3.  Who are the "energy vampires" in your life, and what are you willing to do to make those relationships different? What are you tolerating?

# Go with the Ebb & Flow

*"Nature often holds up a mirror so we can see*
*more clearly the ongoing processes of growth,*
*renewal and transformation in our lives."*
Mary Ann Bussat

Do you experience ease and flow in your life? Are you at peace with where your life is, or do you constantly worry, try to force the answers or attempt to control everything that comes your way? Do you enjoy the rhythm of your life, or are you stressed out, worried, anxious and constantly on the go, even when you don't have to be?

Understanding your own natural rhythm, as well as the natural order of life, can bring not only more peaceful fluidity, but also moments of ecstasy and joy. Our highs and lows in life can convey recognition of what works, what does not work and how to choose more discerning life solutions. Consider the ups and downs of your life path— I suspect there have been happy, peak experiences as well as lonely, confusing disappointments.

No one is immune to difficult circumstances such as a personal illness, feeling low or depressed, a paralyzing ice storm, a financial setback, the ending of a relationship, a difficult co-worker or the deceit of another. But it is in those challenging moments that there are opportunities to have faith, trust, grow, change, transform, evolve, pivot and come back better and stronger than before.

Anne Morrow Lindbergh wrote, "We have so little faith in the ebb and flow of life, of love, of relationships. We leap at the flow of the tide and resist in terror at its ebb. We are afraid it will never return. We insist on permanency, on duration, on continuity; when the only continuity possible, in life as in love, is in growth, in fluidity- in freedom, in the sense that the dancers are free, barely touching as they pass, but partners in the same pattern."

Where does faith and freedom play a role in your life? Find your personal liberty by trusting yourself, following your creative energies, listening to your body and surrounding yourself with advocates. Find a higher faith in God, your Higher Power or the Universe that will sustain, ground and instill hope that all will be well and work out in the end of the rollercoaster ride of life.

Life continues and change is a certainty, so I encourage you to stop attempting to disrupt the natural flow of your life. Learn to trust yourself and move through life with more ease and joy. And if that is difficult at times, I encourage you to examine your beliefs to see if they are empowering and move you forward or are limiting and holding you back. By becoming aware of where you might be stuck, you can start to activate your own energetic flows to create more aliveness, connectivity, creativity and passion.

## Thoughts that Keep You Stuck and How to Turn Them Around:

| Possible Limiting Beliefs to Let Go:<br>TURN…. | New Empowering Thoughts to Create:<br>INTO… |
|---|---|
| 1. Fear | 1. Trusting love |
| 2. Prescriptive expectations | 2. Possibilities & openness |
| 3. Perfection | 3. Balance & boundaries |
| 4. Controlling behaviors | 4. Relinquishing outcomes |
| 5. Limiting beliefs | 5. Inspired actions |
| 6. Mediocrity | 6. Mastery |
| 7. Distracted clutter | 7. Beauty & order |
| 8. Judgment of self & others | 8. Full acceptance |
| 9. Self-consciousness | 9. Vulnerability, self-worth |
| 10. Self-centeredness | 10. Being of service |

| | |
|---|---|
| 11. Headstrong reasoning | 11. Fierce intuition |
| 12. Drama | 12. Peaceful purpose |
| 13. Anger | 13. Motivating passion |
| 14. Caring what others think | 14. Detaching & letting go |
| 15. Making assumptions | 15. Clear communications |
| 16. Regrets | 16. Positive action |
| 17. Guilt & shame | 17. Inner peace |
| 18. Failure | 18. Growth & learning |
| 19. Doing it alone | 19. Creative collaboration |
| 20. Powerlessness | 20. Powerful choices |

Don't allow the spinning tales, made-up stories and unfounded fears hold you hostage in your life. Become consciously aware of your thoughts and be truthful about what is disrupting your life flow. Only then can you seek good intentions and positive change from the ebb and flow of what is given to you each and every day.

## Coaching Questions to Create Flow and Fluidity in Your Life:

1. Do you choose hard or easy?

2. In what ways do you stop yourself?

3. From the above list, choose your biggest limiting belief; think about your behaviors associated with it and then consider the results. To turn it around, work backward by asking, what is the desired result, the desired behavior and then create a new empowering principle.

# Make Space

*"Deep within your soul there is a knowing place...a sanctuary where gifts are nurtured. Enter that space. Spend time there tending your gifts. There in the chapel of your heart, you will become a gift to be given."*
Anonymous

I often hear people say to make space in your life for the things you want. But I sometimes wonder what making space really means and why is it important?

My first thought is that it is about cleaning out the clutter in your physical spaces; getting rid of the things and stuff that no longer work in order to feel more peaceful and have less chaos and clutter. But often, people are simply making room for more, new, different or upgraded things, only to realize months or years later, they have simply accumulated more unwanted or useless material goods that are collecting dust and encumbering a room. The cycle continues, and another clean out is needed.

Clearing the clutter from your physical spaces is needed, but I also believe there are other areas of life where clutter is held and in cleaning that up, it will help you to become freer and lighter overall in life. These other spaces include not only the physical, but also the mental, emotional, relational, financial and spiritual parts. Space, which encompasses all of these areas, is the bigger vision and purpose of your life; the particles are the details, the fears, bad habits, patterns or the things in which people tend to get caught.

So, in order to create a rich, genuine vision that will move you toward all you want, you must be willing to clean up clutter and open space for newness to emerge. It is in the unencumbered places of your body, mind and spirit that you can create an openness to add something new. Learning to embrace the pauses of life, slowing down, staying organized, spacing out for a while, letting go of any attachments, trusting the process, finding happiness with less, and being okay with the unknown are all important to the clean-up process. It is in this stillness and spaciousness that new ideas, people and things can arrive easily and serendipitously, and greater possibilities can be born. Consider what you can do to make room for not only what you deeply desire but also for something better than you could possibly imagine at this point in time.

**Six Life Areas to Free Up More Space:**

1.  **Physical Space** Does your physical environment inspire you or drain you? Simplify, de-clutter and create a personal sanctuary in your home and office. What "things" are you holding on to that you really no longer need, or someone else could use more than you? Donate to charities, non-profits or consignment shops. A consistent business practice I have is when a client moves on to live their authentic journey, I take their file out of my active storage cabinet so that way I make room for new people to engage my services. New people come along at just the right moment in time, so my file cabinet is not over, or under, stuffed.

2.  **Mental Space** What do you think about on a consistent basis? Are you productive, positive and proactive in your thinking, or do you have a tape running in your head over and over again, only to find that you are not really resolving anything, but merely creating a bigger problem instead of truthful solutions? Don't let your unruly thoughts run the show. Get rid of the junk in your mind so that you can be

intellectually engaged and openly stimulated. Clear your mind by doing a brain dump exercise on a regular basis.

3. **Emotional Space** How are you feeling today? Become emotionally intelligent and understand how your emotions drive your thoughts and actions. Learn to name and accept all of your emotions, as they simply are indicators that a change might be needed. Observe them, let them flow through and then use them to create new or different actions.

4. **Relational Space** Do you have positive interactions and deep connections with people who honor you and vice versa? Perhaps you need to recalibrate, rebalance or give someone space so each of you can remain true to yourself. Let go of past relationship issues, defense mechanisms, masks and bad patterns so you can allow more intimacy in a current partnership or make space for a new relationship to blossom. What firm commitment and courageous communication can you make to the people who matter most to you? Take time to have communion with those you love and care for, including yourself.

5. **Financial Space** Do you use your money mindfully? Are you maximizing your hard-earned dollars and being thoughtful with your resources? Do you have debt that creates shame and guilt, or have you become financially dependent on someone else and don't know how to break free? Money is energy, so take the steps to clean up anything that is not positively working for you in this area, such as cutting frivolous spending, saving more, being more generous, creating a financial plan or seeking sound advice.

6. **Spiritual Space** Do you feel connected to God or your Higher Power? Are you making the space to get spiritually

grounded, be in the moment, tap into your intuition, and hear the small voice inside that sheds light in every life situation? Take time to build your faith by getting quiet, praying, meditating, worshipping, cultivating an inner peace, and renewing spirit. Real "inspiration" originates from this spiritual connection.

By making space in your life to deal with the disappointments, the heartaches, the chaos and the clutter, you can make space to re-energize for the necessary work. The Reverend Michael Beckwith said, "We are pushed by our pain until we are pulled by our vision." Deal with any pain or frustration so you can move toward amazing dreams and adventures that are beyond your expectations. Contemplate, imagine, get spaced out, have your head in the clouds, dream with your eyes wide open and make space for your new vision. Remember that by opening up the needed space, you will begin to see what is truly possible.

## A Coaching Exercise for Making Space:

1. If I am at my best, what would this area look and feel like? What do I desire?

2. Where am I suffering or selling myself short?

3. What am I resisting and need to surrender?

4. What would it be like to transcend_____, in order to create_____?

# Experience Your Full Range of Emotions

*"Emotion is the chief source of all becoming conscious.
There can be no transforming of darkness into light
and of apathy into movement without emotion."*
Carl Jung

How are you feeling today? Happy, sad, glad or mad? Can you identify your emotions, many which might be swirling at the same time? Women in particular are often seen as the emotional ones, the backbone of families and organizations. Yet the paradox is that when they fully express those same emotions that make them sensitive, feminine and loving, they are seen as the weaker sex or even incompetent. Women, as well as men, are taught to believe that if they wear their emotions on their sleeves or worse, cry in public, then they are not strong, and are seen as feeble, needy, dependent or even fragile. Further, people are often encouraged to suppress their feelings, to toughen up and to ignore their own needs for the sake of appearing stable, consistent and strong. Is that really an authentic way to live?

In my opinion, emotions are not right or wrong; they are simply a guide to inform you about what you need to do in order to take care of yourself. Understanding your emotional make-up can lead to more successful relationships and deeper connections. But when you ignore your emotions, it can actually intensify the feelings and create a vicious cycle of unproductive thoughts and unclear actions. Suppressing emotional needs can trigger sadness, anxiety, depression, tiredness, isolation, worthlessness and even physical illness. But by truly experiencing your emotions fully and deeply, you can become alive, self-confident, integrated and empowered. By using your emotions to be your trusted inner guide, you will discover how to experience happier and more integrated relationships.

So, can you identify how you are feeling at any given moment? And, if so, do you know what to do with that? The first step is to own your emotions, name how you are feeling and understand how it is impacting you and the people around you. This is part of being emotionally, as well as socially, intelligent. What is often not realized is that you might be experiencing many emotions at the same time so having a savvy understanding of this complexity will allow you to tease out what is really going on.

Next, I think it is important to stay with whatever feeling is there, let it pass and gain the wisdom from that experience. For example, you might get angry every time your boss asks you to stay late at work. It might feel disrespectful and you feel taken advantage of. So perhaps your feeling will empower you to speak up.

Encountering a variety of feelings will allow you to be more sensitive to others, to speed up and keep moving in the direction that feels good or to slow down and take time off when rest or rejuvenation is needed. Having empathy for others, taking inspired action for needed change, stepping into creative solutions or setting boundaries are all part of an emotionally intelligent way of being with emotions. Having an understanding of a deep complex internal state will inform you on how to be happy with whatever is handed to you, it will enable you to be proactive to make desirable and necessary changes.

So, are you letting your emotions have a proper place in your life? Are you learning how your emotions impact you, or are you merely suppressing them and keeping your happy face on, even if that is not how you really feel? Become emotionally empowered and insist on experiencing a full, rich, expressive life. Let's start with identifying as many emotions as you can.

## Enhance Your Life by Honoring Your Emotions:

Listed below are some of the emotions I have unearthed both personally and professionally. In the appendix, there is a more comprehensive list titled "A Sampling of Emotions." With what emotions are you familiar?

| | |
|---|---|
| *Amazed* | *Hopeful* |
| *Angry* | *Hopeless* |
| *Annoyed* | *Hurt* |
| *Anxious* | *Impatient* |
| *Ashamed* | *Inspired* |
| *Blissful* | *Irritated* |
| *Bored* | *Jealous* |
| *Cautious* | *Joyful* |
| *Concerned* | *Lonely* |
| *Confused* | *Loved* |
| *Depressed* | *Optimistic* |
| *Disappointed* | *Overwhelmed* |
| *Ecstatic* | *Proud* |
| *Embarrassed* | *Relieved* |
| *Excited* | *Sad* |
| *Exhausted* | *Surprised* |
| *Frustrated* | *Thankful* |
| *Guilty* | *Tired* |
| *Happy* | *Worried* |

Name, claim and experience as many emotions as possible. Give thought to what learning is available to you and then discover how to be comfortable with whatever arises. Although emotions are fleeting and they do pass, the experience of feeling a wide range of emotions will teach you to be at ease with yourself and others. The more you allow the feelings to flow through you in the present moment, the more plentiful and more relaxed your life can be.

**Coaching Questions to Evoke a Full Range of Emotions:**

1. With which emotions are you comfortable?

2. Take a moment to be with any difficult emotions and consider how circumventing them is a way to avoid pain. What are you doing to escape the pain? (Like shopping, eating, relationships, work, exercise)

3. How do your emotions affect others in your life?

4. If you are not in charge of your emotions, then who or what is running your life?

5. Which feelings would you engage in if you were living your life with more emotional intelligence and empowered awareness?

# Turn Envy into Action

*"It seems to me that we can never give up longing
and wishing while we are thoroughly alive. There
are certain things we feel to be beautiful and
good, and we must hunger after them."*
George Eliot

Do you spend time thinking about what you don't have and what others do have? Do you imagine "the grass is greener on the other side?" Consider what life might look like if you ended up with another person, could be just like so-and-so, could live somewhere else, or perhaps had more money to live a decadently free life? In other words, do you find that you are at times "green with envy" of other people, places and things?

To some degree, I believe most people want more of something they do not have whether it is materially, relationally, spiritually, financially, emotionally or physically. If not, where would the motivation come from to do better, become better, and accomplish more in order to positively impact ours and the lives of family, friends and communities. Envy can provide the desire to create the best version of one's self.

Let's look at the people, places and things you might long for. Instead of envying other people for who you think they are or the life you see that they lead, why not let the things you are attracted to in another person such as their smile, their kindness or their self-confidence, motivate you to find that within yourself or accept your own uniqueness. If you crave being in another place, whether it is a trip or a new home, self-check to determine if you are escaping or running away from a situation you do not want to face or you simply long for more beauty and adventure. When it comes to the coveting of new possessions, buying something because you think it will bring you more overall acceptance or will help you to fit in is not a good reason for your purchase. But if something you want makes you feel beautiful, confident or happy and you can afford it, then go for it.

Unfortunately, as one of the seven deadly sins, envy does have a bad reputation as it can create resentment, jealousy, negativity and keep you stuck. Envy is bad when it hurts your self-esteem, causes you to focus on what you lack, or it creates any negativity around others' achievements. When it causes you to be a victim and makes you feel inferior, you might be compromising who you are. Being a martyr to your circumstances is not pretty either and any of these thoughts can hold you back from creating the life you could have. When you learn to recognize the difference between the good and evil of envy, then envy can inspire you into desired action.

## **Envy is Good When It...**

- Motivates you to learn more about who you really are.
- Crystallizes your own dreams and desires.
- Dismisses mediocrity, inadequacy or fear.
- Teaches you to ask for help from others.
- Encourages you to be real, open, honest and vulnerable.
- Offers a new perspective and viewpoint.
- Ignites authentic action.
- Helps you to find mentors and gain knowledge from their successes.
- Up-levels your work.
- Builds your confidence by making choices that are true to you.

I believe envy can give you the chance to find out what you

truly want. It provides a gauge to see where you rank on your own happiness meter, and it can give you a zeal that creates a drive for a fuller life. Italian poet Dante Alighieri wrote, "Pride, envy, avarice- these are the sparks that have set on fire the hearts of all men." Let envy ignite your desires to turn your jealousy into enthusiastic and rewarding action.

## Simple Coaching Steps to Turn Envy into Action:

1. List the things that you truly envy. Why do you want what you want?

2. Decide what will positively motivate you to move forward and take action based on the right intentions. Are you creating sustainable fulfillment or just happiness in the moment?

3. Now, choose what speaks to your heart and soul and turn that envy into inspired action.

# Know Your Line: Create Boundaries

*"Daring to set boundaries is about having the courage to love ourselves, even when we risk disappointing others."*
Brené Brown

Do you have good boundaries? Do you know how to set them, honor them, and adjust them with the people and situations in your life? It seems to me "boundary" has become a popular buzz word to describe what went wrong in certain situations, yet more definition, self-refection and responsibility might be needed. I often hear the word "boundaries" come up in conversations as a way for individuals to explain a situation, exert power, make a strong point or justify why they are angry, confused or hurt when their lines have been crossed by certain situations or difficult people. Yet, when I think about the purpose of setting a boundary, I wonder if people really understand the purpose of boundaries, when and how to draw appropriate lines, and what it really means for the people on both sides, as well as the individual creating them.

Have you noticed people who set a boundary, whether it's with self or another, only to break the barrier all too quickly? For instance, consider how many new year's resolutions fail, how many people cheat on their diets, how many 3rd, 4th or 5th chances are given to people when they have been betrayed, or how often someone takes a stand on a position or belief, only to give in moments later and participate anyway. People go against themselves hoping they will still be liked, accepted or loved; yet inside, they are betraying themselves, sometimes in small ways when the stakes are not high, and other times when it can be detrimental to how they view themselves. Either way, this self-betrayal chips away at one's soul and the anger towards others is often really a disappointment in one's self. If that's the case, how do you begin to define your own personal boundaries, yet still be able to fully connect and participate with the people and circumstances of your life? After all, what's the point in setting and keeping appropriate boundaries?

Let me start to answer that with a metaphor from one of my life passions. I love dancing; in fact, partner Latin dancing is one of my favorite indulgences. Knowing the steps to salsa, merengue, cha cha, tango and samba are so exciting to me that when I hear a Latin song with a strong beat, I can feel the rhythm in my bones and be confident in being led around the dance floor. Yet, knowing the steps isn't what makes me excel in this pastime... it is being able to hold a boundary and protect my personal space so that I have enough room to "do my thing" and be able to read where my partner is leading me. It can seem counterintuitive to keep the person you want to be close to at a certain distance. However, without this limitation, there would not be enough space to allow for playful spins, complicated steps and free movement. Dancing with a strong container allows me to ground into my body, connect to my partner and have fun moving to music I love. And when both people protect their personal arena, lean into each other's strength and allow a synergistic flow of energy, a mutual respect, self-confidence and powerful connection can emerge.

Boundaries are necessary to preserve the integrity of one's self as well as to teach other people how to treat us. When they are set with compassion, loving-kindness and trust, then everyone benefits. But if you are a silent sufferer and do not remain true to your own set of boundaries, then frustration often results. What seems like anger towards another is often aimed at self. In other words, as Daphne Rose Kingma wrote in her book, *When You Think You're Not Enough*, "Anger is the way we tell other people that they have gone too far, that they've crossed the invisible boundary they shouldn't have crossed if they want to remain in our good graces." Know your line of what is acceptable to you, and what isn't. Boundaries are not meant to be rigid and imprisoning. They are designed to allow you to have more freedom, strength and energy for your own life, and create a healthy connection to another person based on that self-love.

## Six Areas to Consider Setting Decisive, Loving Boundaries:

1. **Personal** I believe everyone gets to decide what they think, what holds meaning, and how they want to portray that in the world. My only caveat: cause no harm to self, others or the world. Do you create goodwill or ill will?

2. **Relational** This area, of course, can the biggest challenge for most people. Our days are filled with relating to others with different needs, wants, desires and expectations in our lives. Be open and upfront with people with what you can and can't do, what you need and how you need it. Co-create with others, and design a relationship that honors both the commonalities, as well as differences. Get comfortable with asking for what you want, and disappointing others. Make sure that you are clear, kind, compassionate and fierce for your own self-preservation— as an individual, parent, child, sibling, spouse, partner, friend, etc. All relationships need boundaries.

3. **Professional** I believe in life balance, not just work/life balance. Right-size not only how much you work, but also how much you think about your career. Create your own rules of engagement for your professional life, set your personal boundaries around your time and decide when and how work needs shows up in your life. I am not suggesting that you do not stay in integrity with a job to be done, but

make sure you create appropriate limitations. And please, use *all* of your vacation and personal time each year.

4. **Financial** Be smart, be informed, ask questions, and build a healthy relationship with money. Save, spend and donate based on what is important to you and your values. Create a clear plan with your resources.

5. **Physical** I believe everyone needs a space of their own that is a reflection of their personal style and is a sanctuary for their soul. It can be a place to reflect, to be creative, to be quiet and to just be. Whether it's an office, a man cave, a special chair or an entire home, this is a must. Additionally, don't let clutter overtake and get in the way.

6. **Energetic** When someone or something drains your energy, you are not obligated to continue to participate. You can express your concern for them and how their dumping is affecting you, suggest professional assistance. And when necessary, remove yourself from the person or situation. There are no victims, only volunteers. Don't be a martyr in your relationships, but rather, choose to spend time with people who lift you up and support you. In other words, go where you are celebrated.

### A Coaching Exercise on Drawing Your Own Personal Boundaries:

Take out a blank sheet of paper, write your name in the middle and draw a large circle around you. This line is your personal boundary. You get to decide who/what gets in and who/what stays out; what is acceptable to you and what is not; what rules are needed and where can there be flexibility.

- Start to think about the people in your life, and the criteria in which they get in the circle. Who is safe? Enhancing?

Energizing? Significant? Supportive? Nurturing? These are the people you want in your circle.

- Who drains you? Causes harm? Sucks your energy? Makes you feel bad? Is unsupportive? Hopefully, these people are outside of your boundary.

- Now consider situations, places, activities, organizations-what are you tolerating? What makes you happy? Is there something you look forward to? Or dread?

Let this inform you as you begin to place the names of people in or out of your circle. You are now consciously and knowingly drawing the lines in your life. Use this visual exercise to guide and support you as you create stronger guidelines for yourself. If you find this is difficult, seek support to talk through what you need and how best be clear with yourself and others.

# What Goes Around Comes Around

*"How people treat you is their karma;*
*how you react is yours."*
Wayne Dyer

In thinking about karma, I have been considering what that word really means. I hear people use the word often, and it appears to me, there are many interpretations floating around. For instance, karma seems to have become pop culture's word for rationalizing the good or bad things that happen to us. I sometimes hear phrases like "It must be karma," meaning destiny or positive outcomes; "That's my karmic debt," implying pre-destination; or "She must have bad karma," signifying bad luck.

According to Dictionary.com, karma is one's fate or destiny. The Western interpretation based on the Christian concept of karma is about "reaping what you sow." A more Eastern approach views the effect of karmic deeds as shaping the past, present and future, as well as the karma representing our "life lesson" or "karmic debt" from something bad that we did in a past life, and we are working off the transgression in this life in order to transform or become enlightened.

Based on the many traditions and modern-day perspectives, it is no surprise that the word "karma" is overused, abused or the catch-all phrase when there is not a reasonable explanation for why something happens. Are people trying to chalk things up to karma as a way of not dealing with issues or to make meaning out of not having enough valid information to discern what is really happening?

Is karma being used as an explanation when people are stuck in life-long patterns such as addictions, relationship issues, money problems and other serious life challenges? Or, does karma make light of what is out of our control?

In my opinion, it does not matter what definition you choose because the point is that karma asks you to change in order to heal. It asks you to take responsibility *now* for your past and present actions, and change your behaviors going forward. To me, karma in its simplest form is about cause and effect; and understanding how your choices impact not only your life path, but also other people around you.

You are in charge of your current thoughts, beliefs, decisions and ultimate actions; there is a natural consequence for your choices. You have the power to determine what kind of influence you want to have—good or bad—on yourself, others and the world at large. What goes around comes around, and you are fully responsible for changing your patterns, determining the quality of your relationships, deciding what your life can look like and how your destiny will unfold. Here are some ways to conduct more conscious deeds.

## Take Responsibility for Your Actions by...

- telling the truth.
- learning from your mistakes and not repeating them again.
- causing no harm to others.
- saying what you really think, want and need by expressing your feelings.
- self-checking your real intentions and motivations.
- not making excuses or blaming others when you really have a part.
- loving without attaching or judging.
- being compassionate.
- not projecting your pain on others.

- letting go of false expectations.
- releasing the outcomes.
- asking for help when you need it.
- practicing forgiveness.
- treating others as you want to be treated.
- setting realistic boundaries.
- wanting more for others than for yourself (it comes back to you!)
- admitting your failures and starting over, if needed.

In his book *The Four Agreements*, Don Miguel Ruiz offers four simple, yet powerful, ways of creating personal freedom, responsibility, and ultimately, true happiness. Be Impeccable with your Word, Don't Take Anything Personally, Don't Make Assumptions and Always Do Your Best... these Four Agreements, when applied, can assist in creating positively powerful thoughts and behaviors. It is up to you to take full karmic responsibility for what happens next. After all, what goes around does indeed come back around sooner or later.

## Purposeful Coaching Questions to Help Change Your Behaviors:

Create awareness and begin the process of change by answering the following questions. If you cannot move forward on your own, always seek outside help through therapy, coaching or a 12-step program.

1. In what life patterns are you currently stuck? What is creating your reality today?

2. What behaviors do you tend to keep repeating, never fully making the necessary changes or tough decisions to affect lasting change?

3. Make a list of everything about which you are resentful. Now consider your "part" in each item you identified. In what ways are you angry at yourself? Perhaps you are going against your values, or not using your voice.

4. What is a powerful interpretation of your current situation or dilemma? And, what is the positive result you want to create?

5. It is time to let go of the past, forgive yourself and others, and make intentional changes to your behaviors. Decide how you can act accordingly.

# Get Busted: The Gift of Failure

*"Failures, repeated failures, are finger posts on the road to achievement. One fails forward toward success."*
C. S. Lewis

I have been told that people must fail, sometimes many times, before success can be attained. There are countless stories of people who have been rejected, lost their fortunes, were told they would not amount to anything or have failed relationships, only to overcome the obstacles and find enormous success in the aftermath. So, if failure is part of the formula for success, why are people so afraid of getting busted?

Society is eager to define what success means for people, and each stage of life seems to be judged by what we do or do not do; have or do not have; and accomplish or do not accomplish. Many people fail along the way, and there seems to be harshness and judgment of those individuals in that moment. No wonder people are afraid to fall short. They are so busy worrying about what people might think that they often miss seeing the gift that failure has to offer. They are running scared from the fear of failure, sometimes more than the failure itself.

So, what's the solution? Fail. Fail fast, fail hard and then tap into a deeper desire to excel and begin again. It has been said that in order to succeed, your desire for victory must exceed your fear of failure. There is a richness and wisdom to someone who has failed and come back with inner strength, disciplined determination, gentle compassion and the knowledge that they can survive adversity.

Henry Ford realized this when he stated, "Failure is simply the opportunity to begin again more wisely."

Allow disappointment to bring you back to your true essence by stripping away any inauthentic expectations, rediscovering your solid values and going forward with what really matters most to you. When my marriage failed, it became an opportunity for me to redefine who I am and then create a career based on what really mattered to me— empowering others to be their true selves. It's probably not something I would have done without failing in the life I had created and then getting honest about what was really important to me. I had to overcome the fear of not being able to support myself emotionally, spiritually and financially in order to move forward with a new life vision.

So, have you gotten busted lately? Has the possibility of failure entered your world and you are afraid of what will happen next? Are you shy about making a mistake, one so big that you might not survive the consequences or perhaps know what to do next? Use this opportunity to discover something bigger and better about yourself. Oprah Winfrey said, "Think like a queen. A queen is not afraid to fail. Failure is another steppingstone to greatness." I urge you to face any fear, embrace failing often so that you can wildly exceed your own expectations and receive the full benefits of living a complete life with meaning, purpose, pleasure and greatness.

**<u>Tips on Embracing Failure:</u>**

- Accept that failure is part of the process.
- Don't play the blame game– don't run or hide from your mistakes but rather clean up what is necessary.
- Make the action wrong, as opposed to the person being wrong.
- Love the lesson itself.
- Apologize for what you did, not for who you are.

- Choose staying positive with others by not spreading negativity, even during the disappointment.
- Be vulnerable and be human.
- Refute any shame or guilt.
- Model failing gracefully and notice your positive personal impact.
- Be flexible and open to change.
- Draw conclusions but don't make assumptions without knowing the facts first.
- Assess rather than judge.
- Be proactive around solutions as opposed to being reactive to fear or pain.
- Create something new and wonderful from the learning, rather than staying stuck in past or pity.
- Don't continue the insanity by doing the same thing repeatedly.
- Look to what you did right; there are always positives.
- Determine what is next and don't stay stuck in the muck.
- See all of the possibilities and make conscious choices.
- Recover and begin again.
- Trust yourself, especially in the unknown.
- Resist shutting others out.
- Ask for help— it is a sign of strength and courage, not weakness and fear.
- Stay connected to your heart, to others and to your bigger vision.

In her Harvard commencement speech in 2008, the Harry Potter series author JK Rowling stated, "The knowledge that you have emerged wiser and stronger from setbacks means that you are, ever after, secure in your ability to survive. You will never know yourself, or the strength of your relationships, until both have been tested by adversity." Welcome the opportunity to get busted and use it as opportunity to continue to transform into the real you. Even

Buddha said, "The only real failure in life is not to be true to the best one knows."

### Coaching Questions to Go from Failure to Empowerment:

1. What is it to transcend your sense of failure?

2. What matters most to you now?

3. What would you attempt to do if you knew you could not fail?

# Go Beyond Illusions: What's Real?

*"Reality simply consists of different points of view."*
Margaret Atwood

We all live in our own reality. We see the world through our lenses-bringing our thoughts, feelings, perspectives, history, experiences, outlook, perceptions, assumptions, habits, strengths, and yes, judgments. We constantly judge, "Is this good or bad? How do I line up or compare to others? Am I doing "it" right? We search for meaning, an "okayness," with our piece of life questioning, "What is authentic and real?" Our reality is just that, *our* reality and what is true for us.

Often, we live our lives in an illusion, creating a story line from what we want to believe or to have happen next. For example, in the dating world, one might believe that a person is really into another because they spend a lot of time dating. That person might think they are getting serious, when the other might only want to have fun and not intend to create a serious, committed relationship. I call this "Illusionary Love" when one person believes real love exists between two people when in reality, it is the hope that love will happen, and they are projecting that desire. What is real or what is an illusion? Each person must decide that for himself or herself.

When it comes to reality, everyone creates his or her own self-perspective. Many of us define ourselves by what the outside appears to look like—successful or struggling, being validated or not, wealthy or poor, "having it together" or still searching. We also spend a great deal of time in either the past disappointments or the future dreams, and we forget to be present to what is happening in that moment. When we allow these external forces, people and situations to determine what is fitting for us, we often come up short. It is only when we move inside that we can relax into what is real, good, whole and true for us in the here and now.

I believe we know what is legitimate for ourselves, but we must get past the illusions, the old stories and the limiting beliefs in order to not only discover whom we truly are but also absolutely live out our essence. One of the aspects I love most about the coaching model is that it allows people to sit in their truth. My job as a coach is simply to ask provocative, thoughtful questions to assist my clients in discovering their own solutions from within their hearts and minds. They must find their way based on their truths, their viewpoints, their genuine beliefs— not mine When they are honest about who they are and free themselves from their self-imposed limitations then they can be inspired to live authentically and act in a genuine way.

Many years ago, I read two books that profoundly changed the way I think and see my reality. The first is *Loving What Is* by Byron Katie where she challenges her readers to ask themselves the question if they can really know something is true or not; and then she gives them a way to turn around their thinking. The second book is Don Miguel Ruiz's *The Four Agreements A Practical Guide to Personal Freedom*. In it he wrote, "God is life. God is life in action. The best way to say, "I love you, God," is to live your life doing your best. The best way to say, "Thank you, God," is by letting go of the past and living in the present moment, right here and now. Whatever life takes away from you, let it go. When you surrender and let go of the past, you allow yourself to be fully alive in the moment. Letting go of the past means you can enjoy the dream that is happening right now."

What dream do you live in? What is real for you today? Does your current life reflect what's deeply inside? For me, I have spent the past decade understanding and creating my reality… here are some of the truths I use to guide me on my journey. I offer these to you, so take what you want and leave the rest.

## My Truths:

- I know I am creative, resourceful, strong and whole.
- I know I am and will be okay, and that God will never give me more than I can handle. (Well, at least I try to remember this, even though it does not always feel this way.)
- I know that feelings are not facts, but rather are indicators of something I need to be aware of. (Is this emotion telling me I need something different? Am I projecting my own stuff onto someone else?)
- I know that I am always in choice about how I feel and the perspective I hold. And, I can choose another one if I want. (What would be a more powerful viewpoint of what is happening in this moment?)
- I believe our thoughts create our reality, and we can be our own master manifesters. When my vision is crystal clear for me and I am inspired, I can take actionable steps.
- I know I only have to do the next right thing, every step of the way.
- I believe in the Four Agreements simple guidelines to living of being impeccable with my word; not taking anything personally; not making assumptions; and always doing my best.
- I know I must be around people who give me energy, not take it away. I love positive, energetic and expansive minds.
- I believe in being of service.
- When faced with challenges, I try to see the good in all people and situations. I ask myself, "What is the learning available in this moment?"
- I know I am responsible for getting my own needs met, yet I can ask for others to assist with that.

- I know it is important to cause no harm to others.
- I know my reality is not the same as others' perceptions.
- I love being in my dreamy, imaginative world. It's from that place that I can create my reality.
- I believe in faith and trust, even when I cannot know for sure. I do not need to see it to believe it. (or hear, taste, smell or feel— although the validation can be nice.)
- I know fear is not real. Yet I wish fear did not feel so real, nor have the big impact is often does. Fear is simply "false evidence appearing real" which keeps people scared, from being fearless and from moving forward.
- I believe, "It's all made up." ™ (Thank you fellow coach Rick Tamlyn who taught me this.) So, if that is true, how do I want to play today? I get to decide.
- I believe the best way to live is by honoring my values and strengths. It creates personal fulfillment and the desire to offer what I have to the world.
- I know my creativity is valid, and important to keep alive.
- I believe gratitude and forgiveness heals.
- I know the outcome will be the outcome. I just need to do my best along the way.
- I believe everyone has the right to be authentically himself or herself, be loved and be happy.

These beliefs are my reality, but they might not be yours. I challenge you to create your own list of beliefs, knowing others might not agree. Believe in for yourself and what you will take a stand for in the world and with others. Determine what is real for yourself and live that in the world. As the late author Wayne Dyer wrote, "Everything you need you already have. You are complete right now, you are a whole, total person, not an apprentice person on the way to someplace else. Your completeness must be understood by you and experienced as your own reality."

### Some Questions to Consider:

1. What are you currently seeking externally that you can look within to receive? (Some ideas: respect, validation, or love?)

2. What parts of your life are you living for other's approval that perhaps you need to stand in your own truth? (It can be as simple as always deferring to your spouse, co-workers, friends or family and ignoring your own needs or as big as have chosen a career because it was either expected or more prestigious, but not really what you originally wanted to do.)

3. Are your beliefs empowering and move you forward or limiting and hold you back? Can you refute the negative impact and choose differently?

4. Ruiz also states, "You can have many great ideas in your head, but what makes the difference is the action. Without action upon an idea, there will be no manifestation, no results, and no reward." What vision do you currently hold that you can truly manifest into reality? What steps would you need to take to make this happen?

# It's the Small Things

*"One of the greatest resources people cannot mobilize themselves is that they try to accomplish great things. Most worthwhile achievements are the result of many little things done in a single direction."*
Aristotle

We often hear "It's the little things in life that matter most." Those small remembrances or thoughtful gestures are what really count and make the biggest difference in life. Yet, it is easy to get caught up in the big stuff— creating a successful business or trying to get that next promotion, finding the perfect partner, being the best parent, building wealth, designing the ideal home, publishing a book, perfecting the body. When attempting to achieve our dreams, the small day-to-day acts of kindness are sometimes quickly dismissed, easily forgotten or completely overlooked. In trying to achieve those soulful aspirations, the people and things we care most about often get ignored, sidelined or even dismissed.

There is nothing wrong with setting out to accomplish great things, but the journey along the way matters. And, you might just get there quicker and more graciously by paying attention to the details. It's like trying to run a marathon. If you have trained slowly and steadily over a period of time, you can achieve it more easily and with less damage to your body than if you just go out and run 26 miles the first time.

I believe in doing the small deeds consistently in order to build trust, stay on track, create sustainability and build ultimate success.

It's the accumulative effect of doing small tasks, and it can be used in most life areas, especially in creating healthy relationships with people, your work, your creativity, your money and your spirituality. Let's take a closer look.

In intimate relationships, people want to feel heard, respected, acknowledged, cared for, appreciated and loved. My clients share with me their desire to receive love letters from their spouses, as opposed to a big piece of jewelry. They are dazzled by daily "I love you's" and other kind gestures on a consistent basis. And, when people do what they say they are going to do and their actions meet their words, it builds trustworthiness. All of these nurturing deposits into the emotional bank account help to build connection, trust and safety, all based on the small acts of love and affection.

In the workplace, people want to hear about their triumphs and to be recognized in small ways, not just at their annual review. It's the validating feedback along the way that will synergize and motivate an employee to keep showing up to give their best, not just a bonus or promotion once a year. Even the smallest recognition can change an attitude, light a fire and brighten someone's day.

In reaching for a goal such as relinquishing weight, saving money or writing a book, the steady, consistent, purpose of an action builds momentum and eventually leads to success. Slow and steady wins the race, especially when a project is large in scope. For example, when writing a book, it takes many drafts and several hours of dedication to create the final product. Sometimes people look for large blocks of time to get it done. In reality, the accumulation of smaller chunks of time every week allowed me to get mine done. The same principle applies to saving money. Making smaller persistent investments earlier on will build more wealth than larger deposits inconsistently. It is the regular installments, disciplined action and commitment to the goal that build up a bank account, whether it's financial or emotional; a full reservoir happens over time.

And finally, faith is built upon a daily practice of spiritual connection and creating a relationship with God, the Universe or your Higher Power. By regularly meditating, praying, journaling, reading, worshiping and learning, you are investing in a relationship that will support you and keep you stronger, grounded and more peaceful during the good times and the bad times as well as transition and uncertainty.

## Small Acts to Lead to Ultimate Success:

All desires can be achieved by the accumulation of doing the small things. Here is a list of "small things" that can make a big difference in yours and others' lives:

- Share positives.
- Smile.
- Say please and thank you, genuinely.
- Show appreciation.
- Praise someone at work for even the small successes.
- Set aside 15-30 minutes each day to work on your dreams or simply journal.
- Practice prayer and gratitude daily.
- Buy for other's preferences, not yours.
- Be gracious.
- Say "I love you" to someone every day.
- Listen actively without fixing.
- Give without expecting recognition.
- Send handwritten thank you notes.
- Pay for the person's coffee behind you in line.
- Send flowers for no reason.
- Give it your best.
- Be generous with your time, money and energy.
- Tip extremely well.
- Say you are sorry first.

- Be of service to others.
- Do something uncomfortable for the sake of helping another person or cause.

Not only do we achieve our dreams by consistently doing the small things, but we also become better people as well. We are the sum accumulation of all of our experiences, good and bad, big and small, pretty and ugly. Take the opportunity to grow, learn and transform and let nothing be wasted. As Aristotle said, "We are what we repeatedly do. Excellence, therefore, is not an act but a habit."

## A Coaching Perspective and Exercise:

The accumulative effect will make your vision doable, attainable, peaceful and enjoyable. Feeling like there is success along the way will give you the inspiration to keep going.

1. What are you investing in, big and small?

2. In what ways are you showing small acts of kindness?

3. Pick Three. With this method, do three tasks per weekday, 15 items per week, 60 per month, 180 per quarter and 720 action items per year. Imagine what 15-30 minutes per day devoted to your vision can do!

# Honor Your Life Cycles

*"No road is too long for him who advances slowly and does not hurry, and no attainment is beyond his reach who equips himself with patience to achieve it."*
Jean de La Bruyere

How do you honor the cycles of your life? Do you give adequate leeway for the necessary stages of growth and completion to occur? Can you stick with the ups and downs, ebbs and flows... for the sake of a full and satisfying life? In today's impatient world of hurriedness and instant gratification, there is an opportunity to slow down, be fully present and savor each stage of the journey. And, when the cycle is complete, honor what has been learned, and then start again.

I like the idea of cycles such as the four seasons or a four-year program because they allow for an extensive period to take place, thereby allowing optimum growth and learning. There is a natural order in life so that whatever is being created can come to fruition, fully mature and then set the stage for the next phase. There must be enough time and space for something to incubate, unfold, grow, develop, change, ripen and be established. By experiencing a complete cycle, it will bring the truest form of what is being created. This must occur in order for there to be fullness, understanding, sustainability and gestation of life.

Let's examine this further. We see this in nature with the four seasons— a time to plant, grow, harvest and rest. An Olympic athlete spends four years training and developing their physical, mental and emotional selves in order to compete at their personal best level. Time is needed to create good habits, peak performance levels and a flow and rhythm to their specific sport. Not only are they training to be at their highest individual levels but sometimes also working together to grow as a team.

A student needs four years of higher learning so the body, mind and spirit can develop and evolve. There is a progression of learning that takes place on many levels, not just the education itself. During their studies, students deepen their knowledge of the basic subjects of reading, writing, math, foreign languages, history, the humanities and sports. But more importantly, they are learning a sense of responsibility and commitment, the development of self-confidence and self-esteem, the endurance of hard work, the value of honesty and integrity, the necessity of organization, the freedom of creativity and the expansion of critical thinking and leadership skills. They are preparing for the next life phase.

Like the seasons, athletes and students, individuals also go through normal life stages. Those who engage in purposeful self-growth processes such as coaching or therapy are more likely to maximize their personal evolvement and create life changes that stick when they allow the full process to happen. By allowing time and space to fully complete a life transition, reach a goal or change a behavior, fulfillment, joy and sustainability can be achieved. The coaching process is best when there is a full sequence of evaluating the starting point, setting intentions or goals, excavating a plan, implementing inspired action, evaluating the results, recalibrating the path and starting again. Each step must be acknowledged and honored.

As novelist Katherine Anne Porter wrote, "There seems to be a kind of order in the universe, in the movement of the stars and the turning of the earth and the changing of the seasons, and even in the cycle of human life. But human life itself is almost pure chaos. Everyone takes his stance, asserts his own rights and feelings, mistaking the motives of others, and his own." Be in charge of your final destiny by choosing to grow along the way and honor your process, including end points and completions.

## Tools for Achieving Completion and Finalization:

- Know your starting point
- Decide your destination or desired final outcome
- Put an action plan in place
- Get going and try something, anything
- Slow down
- Observe and evaluate
- Process along the way
- Savor the journey
- Learn from your mistakes
- Adjust your plan
- Begin again
- When complete, fully honor the achievement, celebrate

## Coaching Questions for Completion:

1. How far have you come?

2. What do you want to complete?

3. What are you learning about yourself?

4. Who are you becoming?

5. How do you want to transcend?

6. What is it to live life fully?

7.  Who are you impacting or influencing?

8.  What is your gift to the world?

9.  What have you built and what is your legacy?

10. How will you honor this completion?

# Conclusion

*"There is more in us than we know. If we can be made to see it, perhaps, for the rest of our lives, we will be unwilling to settle for less." – Kurt Hahn*

**The True You Reimagined** is meant to be a continued catalyst from my original book *The True You* to assist you in becoming your best by following six simple steps: uncover your authenticity; cultivate balance & being; pursue passion & play; enhance your work; enrich your relationships; and break free. I believe it's important to excavate who you are while creating the life you want. And, whether you've lost your way or temporarily lost your confidence, it's time to reconnect with your passion and true essence, and to re-acquaint yourself with what you find irresistible and meaningful.

None of this information will serve you if you do not integrate what you have learned and make the desired changes to your life. Leo Tolstoy said, "True life is lived when tiny changes occur." I hope that what you have uncovered along this journey will inspire you to take the steps needed; and that you will find boundless courage to reimagine the truest you and to live your best life every day in every way possible.

So, I ask you, what are you waiting for? There is no time to waste not living your most fabulous life. Visit **The True You Reimagined** often and for a deeper dive, use **The True You Companion Workbook**. And if you are unable to move forward on your own, I hope you will consider investing in your own incredibly supportive Life Coach.

And finally, I would love to hear about your success stories on how you have reconnected to your true self— big or small, easy or hard, with grace or chaos… they are all part of the big story of your life. Feel free to share with your experiences me at jennifer@ excavive.com.

# APPENDIX

# A Sampling of Values

| | | |
|---|---|---|
| Achievement | Flow | Participation |
| Accomplishment | Freedom | Passion |
| Acknowledgment | Friends | Peace |
| Adventure | Fun & Play | Performance |
| Arts & Culture | Growth | Personal Power |
| Authenticity | Happiness | Positivity |
| Balance | Harmony | Present Moments |
| Beauty | Honesty | Romance |
| Belonging | Honor | Recognition |
| Collaboration | Independence | Resilience |
| Comfort | Impacting Others | Respect |
| Community | Inspiration | Responsibility |
| Compassion | Integrity | Safety |
| Competition | Intensity | Self-expression |
| Connectedness | Joy | Self-love |
| Contribution | Justice | Service |
| Courage | Kindness | Spirituality & Faith |
| Creativity | Laughter | Strength |
| Determination | Learning | Stylish |
| Directness | Loyalty | Success |
| Elegance | Love | Tradition |
| Empowerment | Nature | Trust |
| Excellence | Nurturing | Validation |
| Experiences | Order | Vitality |
| Fairness | Partnership | Wisdom |

# PERMISSION SLIP

I give myself permission to:

*What* _____

_____

_____

*When* _____

_____

_____

*With Whom* _____

_____

_____

*Signature* _____

## Excavive

**Jennifer M. Blair**
Life Coach · Speaker · Author

# A Sampling of Emotions

Accepted
Admired
Affectionate
Amazed
Amused
Angry
Annoyed
Anticipation
Anxious
Ashamed
Awed
Blissful
Bored
Calm
Cautious
Concerned
Confident
Confused
Contempt
Content
Courageous
Defeated
Delighted
Depressed
Despair

Disappointed
Disgusted
Distracted
Doubtful
Ecstatic
Elated
Embarrassed
Empathetic
Enraged
Envious
Excited
Exhausted
Fearful
Frustrated
Grief
Guilty
Happy
Helpless
Hopeful
Hopeless
Hurt
Impatient
Inspired
Irritated
Jealous

Joyful
Loathing
Lonely
Longing
Loved
Nervous
Optimistic
Overwhelmed
Pleasure
Powerful
Powerless
Proud
Relaxed
Relieved
Remorseful
Sad
Satisfied
Serene
Shame
Shocked
Shy
Stressed
Thankful
Tired
Worried

# About the Author

From embracing every moment of motherhood and community involvement to surviving a heartbreaking divorce and reinventing herself with a career she loves today, Jennifer Blair knows how frightening and thrilling change can be. So, in 2003, she founded Excavive™ Coaching & Consulting in Louisville, Kentucky as a way to empower people to pursue their passions, increase their self-confidence, communicate powerfully and build the kind of lives they truly want to live.

Jennifer states, "By embracing my values and my authenticity, I was able to map out my own mission to be of service to others..."

- To be an empowering and enlivening force for women globally to live authentically and beautifully.

- To excavate and activate the true spirit in women, personally and professionally, through coaching, teaching, speaking and writing.

- To lead groups of people to synergistically be their best together with heart, passion, purpose and strength.

Her extensive coaching and leadership skills, as well as personal experiences, allow Jennifer to create compassion and trust with her clients to move them forward to envision and embrace their definition of success. Her passionate commitment to her work focuses on personal and professional coaching, life transitions, creative and entrepreneurial consulting, and inspirational speaking.

Jennifer published her first book, *The True You: Tools to Excavate, Explore & Evolve,* in January 2012, and is always working on her next creative venture. Fueled by the desire for intense joy, ignited by her passionate pursuits and motivated by making a positive impact on others, Jennifer strives to live her life with balance, purpose and passion each and every day, and she inspires her clients around the country to do the same.

# Excavive™ Coaching & Consulting

Jennifer offers several avenues for both personal and professional growth through her company, Excavive Coaching & Consulting—all to help you create the life you have always wanted to live. Whether it's through the Excavive life coaching process of self-discovery, the inspirational speaking events and trainings, or the creative yet practical books she has written, all services assist her clients in confidently and fiercely moving forward in their lives. She specializes in the following:

For individuals at any age and stage of life:

- Life Coaching
- Life Transition Coaching
- Creative & Entrepreneurial Consulting
- Effective & Powerful Communications

For executives and emerging leaders, corporations, non-profits, universities, boards of directors and groups of all sizes:

- Leadership Coaching
- Leadership Trainings
- Inspirational Speaking
- Interactive Workshops

For a free e-book titled, *Be Who You Are: 6 Ways to Excavate Yourself* and a subscription to her newsletter, "Excavate Yourself" sign-up directly on the web site, www.excavive.com. There you will find coaching tips, client success stories, products, upcoming appearances and additional Blog writings. Additionally, to take a deeper dive into self-discovery, look for *The True You Companion Workbook*, to be released Summer 2020. Learn more about any of the Excavive services, including coaching packages or membership opportunities, by visiting the web site, www.excavive.com or connecting directly by e-mailing:

Jennifer Blair
jennifer@excavive.com
www.excavive.com
Louisville, Kentucky

Printed in the United States
By Bookmasters